How to Use the Equity in Your Home or Business Today to Invest for Tomorrow

By Kristie Lorette

With Foreword By Brandon Roe, ***www.23percentplus.com***

HOW TO USE THE EQUITY IN YOUR HOME OR BUSINESS TODAY TO INVEST FOR TOMORROW

1405 SW 6th Avenue • Ocala, Florida 34471 • Phone 800-814-1132 • Fax 352-622-1875
Web site: www.atlantic-pub.com • E-mail: sales@atlantic-pub.com
SAN Number: 268-1250

Library of Congress Cataloging-in-Publication Data

Lorette, Kristie, 1975-
How to use the equity in your home or business today to invest for tomorrow / Kristie Lorette.
p. cm.
Includes bibliographical references and index.
ISBN-13: 978-1-60138-139-2 (alk. paper)
ISBN-10: 1-60138-139-5 (alk. paper)
1. Real estate investment. 2. Financial leverage. 3. Home equity loans. 4. Investments. I. Title.
HD1382.5.L67 2010
332.6--dc22
2009047139

PROJECT MANAGER: Erin Everhart • PEER REVIEWER: Marilee Griffin
INTERIOR DESIGN: Samantha Martin • COVER DESIGN: Meg Buchner
BACK COVER DESIGN: Jackie Miller • millerjackiej@gmail.com

Printed on Recycled Paper

Printed in the United States

We recently lost our beloved pet "Bear," who was not only our best and dearest friend but also the "Vice President of Sunshine" here at Atlantic Publishing. He did not receive a salary but worked tirelessly 24 hours a day to please his parents. Bear was a rescue dog that turned around and showered myself, my wife, Sherri, his grandparents Jean, Bob, and Nancy, and every person and animal he met (maybe not rabbits) with friendship and love. He made a lot of people smile every day.

We wanted you to know that a portion of the profits of this book will be donated to The Humane Society of the United States. ***–Douglas & Sherri Brown***

$2,000
$2,000

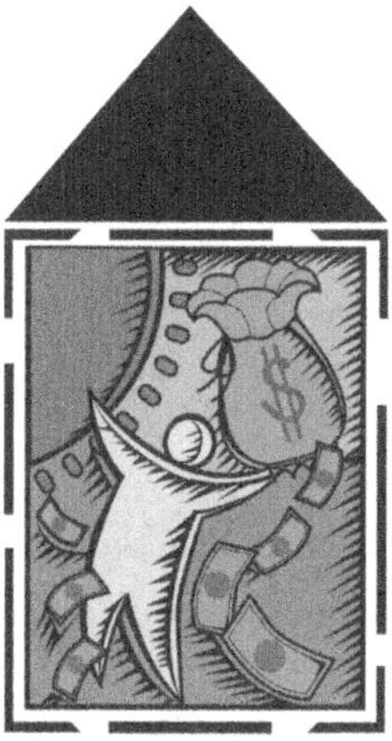

DEDICATION

For my loving parents, whose support and encouragement made me the strong and independent person I am today.

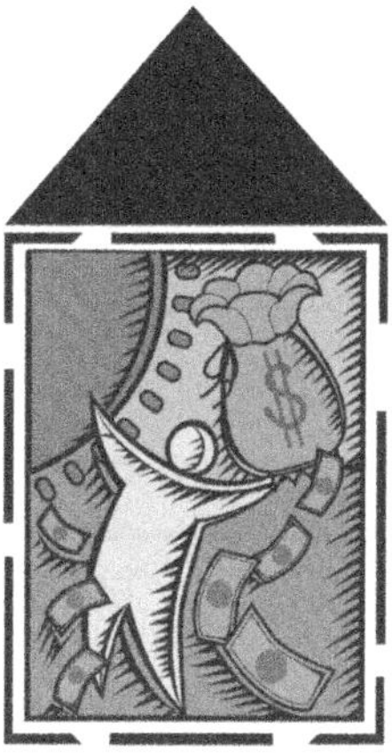

TABLE OF CONTENTS

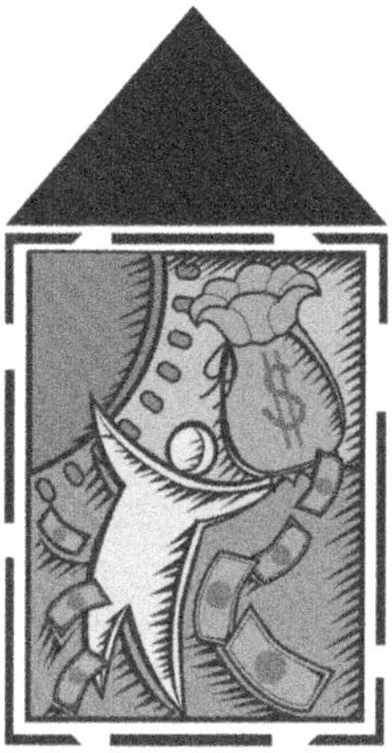

FOREWORD

Over the past 10 years, I have had the opportunity to be around truly successful real estate investors – both as an insider working behind the scenes to help put their deals together and as an outsider looking in and seeing the amazing returns these investors were able to pull out of thin air. These are the real wheelers and dealers who can take properties no one sees any value in and turn them into viable, profitable concerns.

But I have also known many newbie investors who are just getting started. These are the ones who have some equity built up in their home and want to find a way to use that money to create financial freedom through increased net worth.

It is for these people that this book was written.

How to Use the Equity in Your Home or Business Today to Invest for Tomorrow is a must-have book for all those individuals who realize that there is value trapped in their home but do not yet know how to make it work for them. By the time you are finished reading this book, you will know exactly what to do.

It is written in an easy-to-understand format that can take someone who has never heard of terms like "passive income," "built-up equity," and "cash-out refinance" and give him or her everything needed to know to release that trapped value.

You will be guided, step-by-step, through the process of identifying how much equity you currently have in your property, how to free that equity up, and ultimately, the vehicles available to have that equity give you a solid return – whether that be through stocks, bonds, mutual funds, business, private mortgages or, my personal favorite, real estate.

While the content is designed to be both a valuable and engaging first read, you will want to keep it around as a reference guide in the future.

Perhaps best of all, this book is specific enough to satisfy even the most analytical reader out there. Kristie Lorette has spent just the right amount of time talking about "the numbers" through actual scenarios that demonstrate how a strategy will play out in real life.

Add that to the numerous examples, cash histories, and a worksheet or two, and *How to Use the Equity in Your Home or Business Today to Invest for Tomorrow* is definitely a book to add to your library.

Brandon Roe

Brandon Roe is a professional real estate investor with a specialty in raising capital for many types of deals, ranging from small mobile homes to multi-unit apartment buildings. His deals often return investors upwards of 46 percent on their money for a minimal two-year commitment. For more information, visit his Web site at **www.23percentplus.com**.

The 23%+ Club
High-Return Real Estate Investments

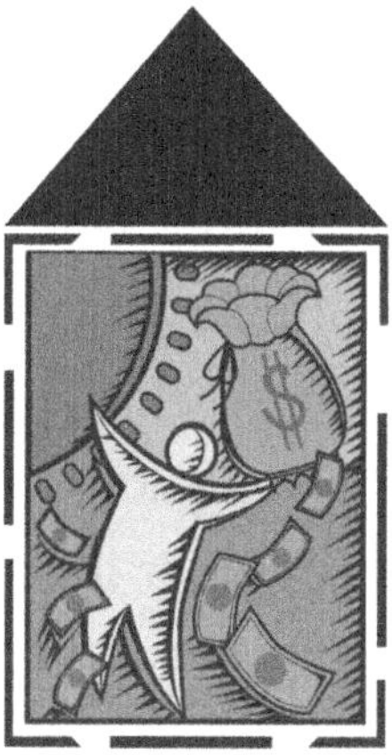

INTRODUCTION

There are many ways to invest your hard-earned money, and what may be right for your friend or neighbor may not be right for you. Investing your money is not only about what is right for your personal financial situation, either; it is also important to consider which investment option(s) will help you meet your financial goals. Whether it is planning for your retirement, creating cash flow and profiting from real estate investments, or buying insurance, it is imperative that you do your homework. Be sure to take the time to thoroughly research your investment options – considering both the advantages and disadvantages – before investing your money into anything. Not only is it important to conduct your own research before making an investment, but it is also important to consider the sources of the money available for you to invest in the first place. You have taken the right first step in researching and investigating one source of money in particular – real estate equity – because you bought this book.

You have to plan for tomorrow today, which also means you have to have money to invest now in order to plan for tomorrow. One of the sources of these funds is the equity you have built up in your real estate property or properties. You can use this equity today to begin building a more stable financial future by investing in additional real estate properties; investing in a stock, bond, and mutual fund portfolio; or funding a retirement account. There are a myriad of additional ways you can spend or invest the money as well. Some of these ways help you to grow and appreciate the value of the money you invested. Others deplete the funds without providing you with a return or by providing you with too small a return on your investment. This book covers the ways you can invest your equity funds wisely — the ways you can grow and enjoy the appreciation rather than the depletion of your investment. It provides you with the information you need to research and learn how to leverage the equity buildup in a real estate property or business to plan for your future, rather than spend it frivolously for instant gratification that does nothing to better your future financial situation.

How to Use the Book

How to Use Equity in Your Home or Business Today to Invest for Tomorrow delves into everything you need to know about leveraging your home and commercial property equity to invest in various types of investments. First, you will learn a great deal about what equity is, how it builds, and the various financing options available for you to access it. After you know everything you need to know about equity, it covers the various investment options you can choose from that ideally earn you a greater return on your investment than leaving it as equity in your property – i.e., sitting on a pile of money.

The first half of the book covers equity and the basic financing options available for tapping into this equity in a property for residential and commercial properties. Once you have a firm grasp of this, you will learn the differences that exist between residential and commercial properties and how this may affect your ability to access the equity. You will also be introduced to the calculations that lenders use to determine how much equity you have in the property – and, more importantly, how much equity they will let you borrow, use, or access.

While the first half of the book covers the basics and helps you build a foundation, each chapter in the second half of the book covers the details of a specific investment option for your equity funds. It is recommended that you read the book in its entirety to build a solid foundation of knowledge about equity and financing, then research the investment options available to you. The second half of the book is an investment reference guide, so you could skip around in this half to go directly to options that interest you. However, to fully appreciate everything your equity can do for you, reading each chapter may open your eyes to a new investment option or one that you have not considered before. This allows you to make an educated decision about the investment before using your equity funds.

At the beginning of each chapter, you will find a bulleted list that provides you with a preview of what will be discussed in the chapter. Checklists, tips, and warnings are scattered throughout each chapter. The tips and warnings on investing your equity funds in the each particular investment discussed helps you to make a decision on whether or not this investment option is a viable one for you. It points out the benefits, as well as the problems you may encounter with each option. Once you decide which investment option is most advantageous to your personal financial situation, the checklists help to guide you through the process of investing your equity money in that investment.

It is important that you keep an open mind as you read through the investment options. After all, you are reading this book because you have an interest in using money that is sitting in a property. The equity you have built up in your property is probably earning you a small return (if you are earning any return at all). It is also a return you will not be able to access until you sell the property or tap into the equity to invest it in a vehicle that produces a greater return. In order to accomplish this goal of using the money, you need to know exactly what you can do with the equity funds. Do not make decisions based on what happened to your family member or neighbor; financial situations and goals vary from person to person. Use the information in this book to gain the knowledge and information you need by learning the benefits and disadvantages for each option. Then, use this knowledge to make a personal decision for what is the right investment option for you.

COUREY-LENTZ
SECRETARY
Trust & Savings Bank
MAIN BRANCH
Y-A 330765

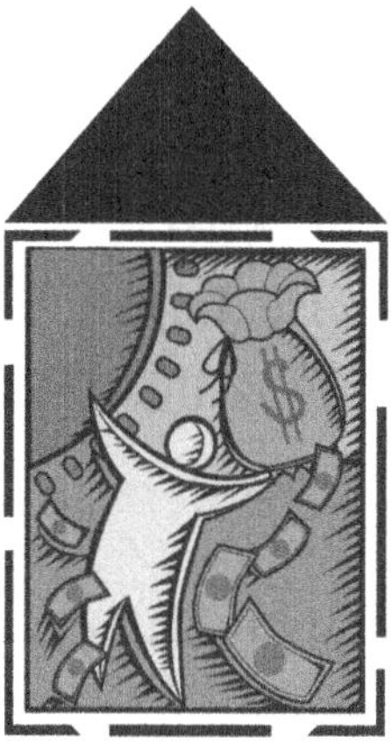

CHAPTER 1

Everything You Need to Know about Equity

In this chapter you will:

- Learn what real estate equity is for residential and commercial properties
- Discover the various ways that equity builds in real estate
- Uncover various ways you can accelerate the equity buildup in your real estate
- Find out how the recent economic downturn and slump in the housing market has affected equity buildup
- Learn how the recent decline in the mortgage industry has affected the financing options available to tap into real estate equity

If you own a real estate property or have been around people talking about real estate, then you have probably heard the term "equity" being thrown around. It may have left you wondering: What exactly is equity? Simply stated, equity is a real estate property's value after reducing the market value by any outstanding mortgage, lien, or other debts owed on the property. Value is a relative term because there are different ways that value is determined. Whether you are talking about a residential home where you live or a commercial property that you rent out, what is valuable to you may not have any value to someone else. In the case of real estate, an official appraisal of the property typically determines the value.

For real property — your home or the commercial building that you own — an appraisal is done by a lender-approved property appraiser in order to assess the value, but there is also a lot of behind-the-scenes work done by an appraiser to determine the current appraised value. This includes comparing your home or building square footage and amenities to the recent sales of similar property in your area. Simply stated, the market value of the property is what you could sell it for today in its current state and condition.

The amount of equity you have built up in your property and the amount a lender will allow you to borrow are usually two different numbers. *Chapter 4 will go into more detail about how lenders calculate the amount of equity you could access.* When it comes down to determining the value of a commercial property or residential property, the process is similar. There are differences in residential and commercial properties, so a lender will use an approved commercial property appraiser rather than a residential appraiser.

In the interest of simplicity, home equity calculations look like this:

Home value	$300,000
Mortgage	- $150,000
Potential equity	$150,000

Potential equity is used here instead of actual equity because this straight math calculation is not how lenders determine the amount of equity they will lend you; it is simply the available amount of equity you have built up in the property. Still, very few lenders will loan you the full amount because the more the lender loans to you, the greater the risk is to the lender. In order to reduce the amount of risk, the lender looks to the loan-to-value ratio, which is the percentage they use to calculate how much money they will lend you based on the market value of the home. Typical loan-to-value ratios for an equity loan or equity line is 80-85 percent on a primary residence, while vacation homes tend to have a loan-to-value ratio of 75 percent, and investment properties tend to be 50 percent (if the lender allows you to pull equity out of an investment home at all). *Chapter 4 goes into detail on how lenders calculate your amount of equity allowed to open an equity line or use another financing option to pull the equity out of the property.*

How Equity Builds

Now that you have an understanding that equity is the amount left over after you deduct the debt from the value of a property, it may leave you wondering how equity builds to begin with. There are various ways that equity naturally builds in real estate property. There are even ways that you can accelerate the equity buildup. One of the most common ways equity builds in a property is when the value increases. This is true even if the mortgage balance you owe on the property remains the same because the difference between the value of the property and the amount you owe increases.

During the 1990s and early 2000s, property values crept up steadily. In some areas of the country, such as Florida and California, property values spiked — increasing at a faster rate and greater value than the typical 1 to 2 percent per year. This spike in property value enabled property owners to access a larger amount of equity than the amount that was available in prior years. These property values during this timeframe increased at rates above 5 percent, with some areas even hitting the double-digits. This is also why these areas of the country — Florida and California, especially — suffered the most during 2007-2009 when the housing market declined rapidly. As we entered the last quarter of 2009, the U.S. stock and housing markets were starting to turn around, with the stock market and housing values beginning to level off and increase. These positive effects are indicators that the U.S. economy is gradually recovering from the recession it has been in since 2007.

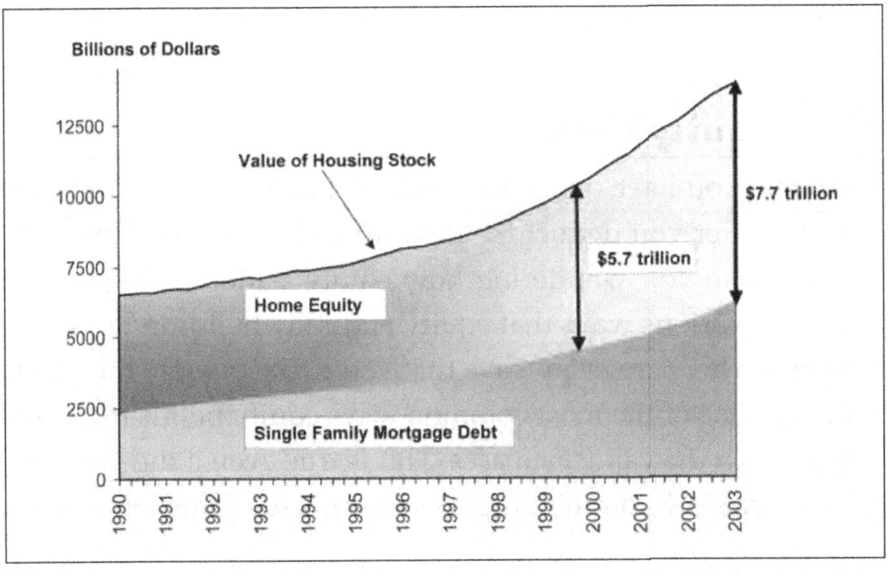

U.S. home equity growth, 1990–2003 (source: Board of the Governors of the Federal Reserve System)

In late 2007, housing values started heading in a downward spiral, which also decreased the amount of equity homeowners had built up in their properties. The decreased value was so drastic that it left many homeowners with greater mortgage balances than their homes were even worth. In high unemployment areas of the United States — like Michigan, where unemployment rates skyrocketed due to layoffs from the auto industry — when the mortgage balance was greater than what the property owners could making from selling, and they could no longer afford to make their payments because of job loss, the home foreclosure rate also reached an-all time high by 2009.

Equity also builds over time, and making mortgage payments on your property chips away at the balance you owe. The amount of equity varies according to the type of mortgage you hold, so certain types of mortgages allow you to build equity at a faster rate than others. For example, a 15- or 30-year, fixed-rate mortgage requires you to pay the principal and interest payments on your mortgage each month. For about the first half of these mortgages, interest makes up the majority of the payment you are making. After you pass the halfway mark, the roles reverse, so now more principal and less interest make up your monthly mortgage payment. As more principal is applied, the balance of the mortgage is reduced, and this also helps to build equity in the property. The less you owe on the property, the more equity you have because the value is surpassing the amount owed.

Paying off debt on the property also increases the equity buildup in your property. For example, if your home is worth $250,000, and you hold a mortgage for $30,000 that you pay off with the bonuses you and your spouse receive, as well as your tax refunds for the year, then the equity in your home increases. Because you no longer have a mortgage or any other lien on the property, you now own it free and clear. This means you have increased the amount of equity in your home by increasing the difference between the value of the property and the mortgage balance.

While there are natural ways that the amount of equity in your real estate grows, there are also ways you can accelerate the equity buildup in your property.

How to Accelerate the Equity Build in Your Property

One way you can accelerate the buildup of equity in real estate is to pay off your mortgage balance early. Hundreds of mortgage lenders and services offer a biweekly payment option, which allows you to make half of your mortgage payment every two weeks and helps you pay off your mortgage earlier than the set term. Naturally, this helps to reduce the mortgage balance faster because you are paying a chunk of interest and a chunk of principal at two separate times, so the interest accruing is less in the long run. Using a bimonthly payment option also equates to paying one extra mortgage payment per year, which also reduces the length of time you hold your mortgage.

Since most mortgage lenders charge a fee to set up the bimonthly payment program, a cost-free option for accelerating your equity is to simply make one extra mortgage payment per year. This extra payment is a direct reduction of your principal balance because none of this payment is applied toward interest. When you make the additional payment by mail, there is a line for you to indicate how much of the additional payment amount should be applied directly to the principal balance. If you make your payment online, you may want to indicate this in a note to the lender, or in the memo of your bill pay area if you make your payment from your bank bill pay service. Typically, any extra payment is applied toward the principal automatically, as long as you are current on your mortgage and escrow payments. Remember, as your debt on the property reduces, the amount of equity in the property increases.

This, too, assumes that the property value stays constant. If the property value and mortgage balance both drop, you will still have equity in the property, but it may not be as much as if the property value remained constant. If the property value increases as your mortgage balance drops, you may have even more equity available than if the property value were constant.

Making one extra mortgage payment per year without using a bi-monthly payment program requires willpower and diligence because you have to make the effort to use additional funds to pay down your mortgage rather than spend the money on a family vacation instead. If you are not diligent enough to make one extra mortgage payment per year, you can also apply extra principal reduction payments with each monthly payment you make. Take your monthly mortgage payment and divide by 12 to determine how much extra you need to pay each month to equal one extra payment. When you write the monthly mortgage payment check or schedule the bill to be paid online, add this extra amount to the amount due. These small extra payments chip away at the principal balance throughout the year and help you to achieve the same result: paying off your mortgage earlier and building your equity faster. It may be easier to pay in small increments each month rather than having to come up with a larger sum at the end of the year.

If you are a commission earner or your company pays bonuses throughout the year, these are other great opportunities to reduce the principal balance of your mortgage and increase the amount of equity in your property. Use some of the money from your bonus or large commission checks to make payments to reduce the principal balance of your mortgage. This permits you to make your extra mortgage payment in full when it is financially available and convenient for you.

The type of mortgage you have also affects how quickly you can build equity in your real estate property. Fixed-rate mortgages, which include your standard 15- and 30-year mortgages, are on a payment schedule that requires a combination of principal and interest payments to be made each month. With standard payments being made each month, it is easy to figure out how much of your payment is toward interest on your mortgage and how much is toward the principal at any time. When you make additional payments or principal reduction payments with a 15- or 30-year, fixed-rate mortgage, you build equity in your home, but your monthly mortgage payment remains the same.

For example, if a 30-year fixed-rate mortgage is established on Sept. 2, 2009, at an interest rate of 7 percent, then using the mortgage payment calculator at BankRate.com (**www.BankRate.com**), the monthly principal and interest payment is $1,097.75. By running an amortization schedule using BankRate.com's Amortization Calculator, you can see that for the October payment (Month

10), $135.25 is applied toward the principal balance of the mortgage and $962.50 is applied toward the interest on the loan.

Month	10	11	12
Year	2009	2009	2009
Payment	1,097.75	1,097.75	1,097.75
Principal Paid	135.25	136.04	136.83
Interest Paid	962.5	961.71	960.92
Total Interest	962.5	1,924.21	2,885.13
Balance	16,4864.75	16,4728.71	16,4591.88

If you fast-forward into the future, using the same loan and the same amortization schedule, it shows that after paying on the mortgage for 15 years (about halfway through the term of the mortgage), $385.32 is applied to the principal while $712.43 is applied toward the interest for Month 10.

Month	10	11	12
Year	2024	2024	2024
Payment	1,097.75	1,097.75	1,097.75
Principal Paid	385.32	387.57	389.83
Interest Paid	712.43	710.18	707.92
Total Interest	15,5438.4	15,6148.59	15,6856.51
Balance	12,1745.81	12,1358.25	12,0968.42

Finally, when you look at the amortization schedule for the last year of the loan, the majority of the payment ($1,023) is now put toward the principal, while $74.01 is being applied to the interest for Month 10.

Month	10	11	12
Year	2038	2038	2038
Payment	1,097.75	1,097.75	1,097.75

Principal Paid	1,023.74	1,029.71	1,035.72
Interest Paid	74.01	68.03	62.03
Total Interest	22,9777.52	22,9845.55	22,9907.58
Balance	11,663.08	1,0633.36	9,597.64

On the other hand, if you have an interest-only mortgage, these types of mortgages allow you to build equity faster because any extra payments you make over the minimum amount due goes directly toward reducing the principal balance of your mortgage. Depending on the terms of your interest-only mortgage, your monthly payment may also be re-calculated based on the new principal balance. This means as your principal balance is reduced your monthly interest payment is also reduced. As you continue to make payments, this means more of your payment is applied toward principal and less interest is due. This also means you are paying less interest on the borrowed amount in the long run.

For example, Susie owns a home worth $150,000, and she has a mortgage on the property for $100,000. With an interest rate of 7 percent, her minimum monthly interest payment is $583.33, calculated by:

Balance of mortgage X Interest rate = Interest per year
$100,000 X 0.07 = $7,000

Interest per year / Months in a year = Minimum monthly interest payment
$7,000 / 12 = $583.33

Rather than making the minimum payment each month, Susie rounds her payment up and pays $1,000 on the mortgage for January. The portion of the payment paid above the $583.33, which is $416.67, is applied directly toward reducing her principal balance of the mortgage. In February, Susie's interest-only payment due is $580.90:

Previous mortgage balance – Extra principal payment = Balance of mortgage
$100,000 – $416.67 = $99,583.33

Balance of mortgage X Interest rate = Interest per year
$99,583.33 X 0.07 = $6,970

Interest per year / Months in a year = Minimum monthly interest payment
$6,970 / 12 = $580.90

In February, Susie pays $1,000, which makes her March payment $578.46. Susie then receives a $10,000 bonus from her job at the end of the first quarter of the year. She decides to apply $2,000 of this to the principal amount of her mortgage. In April, Susie makes a payment for $2,578. This reduces Susie's May payment to $566.79.

Previous mortgage balance – Extra principal payment = Balance of mortgage
$99,583.33 – $419.10 = $99,164.23

Balance of mortgage X Interest rate = Interest per year
$99,164.23 X 0.07 = $6,941.50

Interest per year / Months in a year = Minimum monthly interest payment
$6,941.50 / 12 = $578.46

If you continue this payment behavior over time, it accelerates the buildup of equity in the property. It also shortens the length of time that your mortgage will be outstanding. Again, the shorter the amount of time you have the mortgage balance outstanding, the less interest you pay in the long run. Principal reduction payments on interest-only mortgages combined with increases in property value creates a situation where you build up equity at an even quicker rate than an amortized principal and interest mortgage.

There are also certain property improvements and renovations you can do that help you build up equity in the property at a quicker rate. It is important to note the word "certain" here because there is a common misconception that all home improvements increase the value of the property on a dollar-for-dollar basis. (For example, if you spend $50,000 renovating your home, you add $50,000 of value to your home, which in turn increases the amount of equity available in the property – by how much depends on the type of renovations you have done.) The amount of the increase depends on the type of renovations you do on the home. Typically what adds value to a home is when square footage is added, or previously non-livable areas (such as basements and attics) are finished so that they are turned into livable space. Putting money into home renovations and remodeling to increase the value of your home is a great concept in theory, but it is not exactly how property valuation works. The bottom line is that the increase in value depends on what type of renovations, upgrades, or remodels are made to the property.

What tends to add value to a property is adding square footage to a home or property. For example, if you finish an unfinished basement, it adds square footage to the living area of the home and adds value to the property. Another example is adding a sunroom to your house, which gives you and your family a place to enjoy nice weather and adds value to the property because you have increased the livable space. Again, you will not increase the value of the property dollar for dollar, but adding square footage to a home or commercial building does tend to push the value of the property up and in turn builds more equity into the property.

There are other types of renovations that add value to the property and accelerate the buildup of equity. According to *Remodeling* magazine's 2008-2009 "Remodeling Cost vs. Value Report" produced by Hanley Wood, LLC, renovated kitchens can bring you up to 80 percent of the renovation cost as an increased value in your home, and bathrooms can earn up to 75 percent as an increase in value to the property. However, beware of being fooled into thinking your $30,000 kitchen renovation is going to immediately increase your equity in the property. The appraiser from the company where you are applying for a home-equity loan may give you a couple of thousand dollars in value, but it is not necessarily going to boost your equity by the full $30,000 or even close to it. Typically, your equity increases by approximately 80 percent of the cost of renovation of a kitchen. So if your kitchen renovation cost $30,000, you will generally see an increase in the value of the home of approximately $24,000. You really gain the return on your investment when you sell the home or building.

When it comes to commercial properties (rental apartments, office buildings, and shopping centers, for example), if the owner collects rent from its tenants, they have a natural equity buildup because of the cost-of-living increase that takes place. You typically think of a cost-of-living increase as additional money in your paycheck to cover the higher cost of goods such as food, gas, and rent. In reality, a cost of living increase provided by your employer simply brings your income level up to match the cost of essentials, so the "increase" in your income is canceled out by the higher costs you have to pay to live. Cost of living, however, is also a concept that benefits real estate owners and investors when it comes to rented or leased properties.

The monthly mortgage payment you are required to pay on one of these commercial properties is not affected by the cost of living, but the rent amount you can charge is (or can be) affected. As the cost of living increases, you can raise the rent amounts on these units, which can cause your income or cash flow from these properties to increase, while your monthly mortgage payment remains the same. This, of course, is true only if the expenses for maintaining the property remain the same also. So now you are receiving a greater income payment from the property with the expenses for the property staying the same, so you have more cash flow or equity in your pocket. You can use this additional equity to make additional or increased mortgage payments to pay down the principal balance of the mortgage, which then accelerates the buildup of equity in the property.

Depending on the state laws where you own property, landlords can raise the rent even if your lease is not yet up to expire or for renewal. For example, in California, rent can be raised before a lease is up as long as the landlord gives the tenant 60 days notice before the increase becomes effective. Typically, there are also stipulations included in the lease agreement that state the landlord's right to raise the rent amount and how much notice they have to give to the tenant. While raising rent whenever landlords so desire is probably not common practice or the norm, rate increases before lease expirations do happen; they are legal in some states.

In his book *The Home Equity Acceleration Plan,* Roccy DeFrancesco introduces his concept of accelerating the equity buildup in a property by using H.E.A.P™ in conjunction with a home equity line of credit. This is an interesting approach to building equity, but it is really more of a rearrangement of equity, so the term is somewhat of a misnomer. DeFrancesco suggests that if you use your home equity line of credit to pay down a chunk of your first mortgage in order to cut down on the interest you pay in the long run, then in the process, you will also be cutting the length of time your first mortgage balance is outstanding.

What he does not seem to address is that this simply moves a chunk of money from the first mortgage to the second mortgage. This does not affect the amount of equity you have in the property; it simply moves the position of the balance from your first mortgage to your second mortgage. DeFrancesco admits in the book that H.E.A.P does not change the amount of debt you have outstanding on the property, which also means that the amount of equity in the property has not changed, either. There is more to the H.E.A.P approach that may be a wise choice to pay down your first mortgage quicker, but is not necessarily an option for building equity in the property at a faster rate.

Recent Changes in the Real Estate Market Affecting Equity

When real estate property values skyrocketed in the late 1990s and the early part of the 2000s, it created a situation where many property owners experienced a huge increase in the amount of equity in their home or real estate property. Many of these property owners used this as an opportunity to take out an equity line on the property or to refinance the property in order to pull cash out (access the equity) of the property. The funds received from the property's equity were used for various reasons, including paying for vacations and buying luxury items like boats and expensive cars. Because the interest rates were reasonable at the time, it was also an affordable way to pay off high-interest consumer and credit card debt, make home renovations, or pay for a child's college education. Thousands of homeowners saw their homes as a cash machine rather than as an asset, so they used the funds to buy depreciable assets rather than invest in ways that could benefit them in the future. More than anyone, these homeowners would be the ones who would suffer the most if property values plummeted.

During 2007, the U.S. economy began its journey into a recession, and the fallout of effects of the recession would change the housing market, the mortgage industry, and any companies that cater to the real estate market for years to come. In fact, at the time of press for this book, these industries are still maneuvering through the tumultuous market. Real estate values started to decline, and all of the borrowers that took out a mortgage on an adjustable-rate loan a few years back were now experiencing the adjustment of their mortgage interest rate. Because most of these mortgage rates adjusted up, it also caused their monthly mortgage payment to increase, which meant they could no longer afford to make their mortgage payments. To try to resolve the financial issue, many homeowners put their homes on the market to try to sell them. The problem: When they went to sell the property, they found out that because of the decreased property values, the property was now worth less than what they owed on the mortgage(s) they had on the property. When you owe more on your mortgage than your property is worth, this is called being upside down on your mortgage.

So, there were thousands of homeowners around the country who could no longer afford to make their mortgage payments, and they could not resolve their problems by selling their homes because the sale price they needed was not enough to cover the entire mortgage balance to break even. This caused the lenders that were holding the mortgages on these properties to start foreclosure proceedings; then, foreclosure rates around the country started to spike.

The foreclosure phenomenon gripping the entire country resulted in never-before-seen plunges in real estate values from coast to coast. Some areas of the country were more affected than others. Some of the hardest-hit areas included Ohio, Michigan, Florida, Georgia, Tennessee, and California; because the home values in these areas rose even more sharply than other areas of the country in the late 1990s and early 2000s, bank and mortgage companies began offering loans to homeowners that allowed people to finance these properties with little or no money down. On top of these home buyers' financing up to 100 percent of the purchase price, they were getting an even bigger bang for their buck by using adjustable-rate mortgages (ARMs) to buy these homes. It meant they could afford bigger and more expensive houses because they could finance more with less money out-of-pocket and have a lower monthly mortgage payment with an ARM. The problem, however, reared its ugly head when it was time for these ARMs to adjust. When they did adjust three to ten years after the loan was established, the owners found themselves with mortgage payments that were two to three times the original amount. Faced with these higher payments that they could no longer afford, homeowners started defaulting on their loans. By the thousands, foreclosure rates in communities across the United States skyrocketed.

Foreclosures are bad news for a number of different reasons, on a number of different levels, and for a number of the parties involved – such as homeowners, mortgage lenders, neighborhoods, and municipalities; in the 2009 economy, foreclosures affected the entire country. As of October 2009, the U.S. foreclosure rate was up 23 percent since October 2008, with one in every 136 homes receiving a foreclosure filing, according to a RealtyTrac report. When a mortgage lender forecloses on a property, the lender assumes the deed to the property and takes ownership. At the time the bank, credit union, or mortgage company forecloses on the property, it also has the right to legally remove the owner from the home. Because the mortgage lender is not in the business to own real estate, its main goal is to recoup the funds due. In order to limit its losses, the lender usually resorts to auctioning off or selling the property, typically for pennies on the dollar. As a result, this has perpetuated the low value of real estate properties, causing homes that are not in foreclosure to sell for rock-bottom prices because they are forced to compete with foreclose prices; this drags down the value of entire neighborhoods in cities such as Atlanta, Cleveland, Las Vegas, and Detroit. In these cities, homeowners have helplessly watched as the equity they had built up in their homes plunged dramatically or disappeared completely.

Remember, the value of a home or property is determined by the comparable properties that have recently sold in the area. So, if a comparable property in the area is sold for pennies on the dollar, this affects the value of your property, too. In some instances, there are more foreclosure properties on the market than there are homeowners trying to sell their homes, so it makes the value of real estate even bleaker.

As foreclosure rates increased, it was as though a domino effect took over. With a multitude of businesses and industries related to or serving the real estate and mortgage industries, not only is the real estate market in turmoil, but all of the industries connected to it are also experiencing problems. So, not only were banks and mortgage lenders going under, but home improvement stores, builders, and appliance stores were feeling the ill effects, too.

What began in the residential housing market soon trickled into the commercial real estate industry. Office buildings, retail strip malls, hotels, apartment complexes, and mixed-use residential properties — retail stores on the ground floor and apartments or condos on the floors above — were also dropping in value, causing the equity available in these types of properties to decline. With all of the economic turmoil in the economy, people started to cut back on their spending, which affected all of the businesses that lease, rent, and own these commercial properties. With little or no money coming into the business, many of the businesses occupying these units were forced to close their doors. Now, the owners of these buildings are not receiving rent to cover the mortgage and maintenance of the building, and the problems continued to perpetuate. The owners of the businesses lost their income, and the employees of the closed businesses lost their jobs, so none of them could pay their bills, rents, and mortgages, either.

Despite all of the gloom and doom that the 2008-2009 economic and real estate decline has caused, there is a silver lining. With the steady decline in property values, it became — and still is — a real estate investor or buyer's dream. Properties that they once were not able to afford were now being sold at attainable prices. Real estate investors who buy these properties for various reasons were scooping them up at bargain prices. Buyers who were not able to afford buying homes before were now able to purchase homes for the first time. Coupled with lower sales prices, mortgage interest rates continued to drop, so not only were buyers paying lower prices, they were financing these purchases at low interest rates.

Now the problem is that there are fewer mortgage lenders and banks available to obtain financing for purchases. The lenders that remain standing have more stringent lending guidelines and require higher credit scores and a higher down payment than past buyers experienced. So even if a potential buyer can afford the purchase price of the home now, they may not be able to qualify for the financing because they do not have the credit score to ensure they are qualified to pay back the loan.

As of 2009, not too much has changed in the housing, real estate, and mortgage market; it is still generally bleak. Economic stimulus plans and various bailout programs implemented by the federal government to try to salvage the banks and mortgage lenders around the country have had little impact. There were moments of clarity where the situation seemed to be climbing out of the rut in late 2008 and early 2009 — signs that the market was starting to correct itself with some upward ticks in the stock market and moments when housing prices stopped declining and leveled out or even increased. History shows that when the market and certain industries decline, there is a period when it eventually goes back up. Still, when the real estate industries return to normal or to an advantageous financial situation remains unknown.

Regardless of when the housing and lending market make their comeback, equity is an important asset, and knowing how to effectively manage it is a critical skill. Real estate, like any investment, fluctuates. Nobody knows this better than the property owners that have felt the effects of the recent turmoil. Eventually, real estate values will increase, so the properties in the most devastated cities could see the 30 percent decrease in property value they experienced return to them, and their equity build once again. This will not occur overnight, but over time, real estate and housing market professionals expect housing prices to increase from the current value and return to producing anywhere from a 1 to 2 percent increase year-over-year — as it once was prior to the 2007 decline and the price spikes that took place in the 1990s.

Finding ways to invest your equity wisely is key. As a general rule, avoid sinking money into depreciating investments such as boats, motorcycles, or expensive vacations, especially if you have to draw funds from what is typically an appreciating asset to do so.

Checklist	
✓	Understand what equity is
✓	Do a quick calculation of how much equity you have available to get an idea if this is a viable source of funds to invest
✓	Understand how equity builds
✓	Determine if one of the equity acceleration options is right for you

BALANCE AS SHOWN ON PREVIOUS STATEMENT
TOTAL AMOUNT OF DEPOSITS AND OTHER CREDITS
THIS IS YOUR ACCOUNT NUMBER PLEASE USE ON ALL DEPOSIT TICKETS AND CHECKS
CHECKS AND OTHER DEBITS
VISTA GOLD
NATIONAL BANK
City Trust & Savings Bank
MAIN BRANCH
PAY
City Trust & Savings Bank
MAIN BRANCH
PAY
TO THE ORDER OF
CHECK
BUREAU OF ACCOUNTS

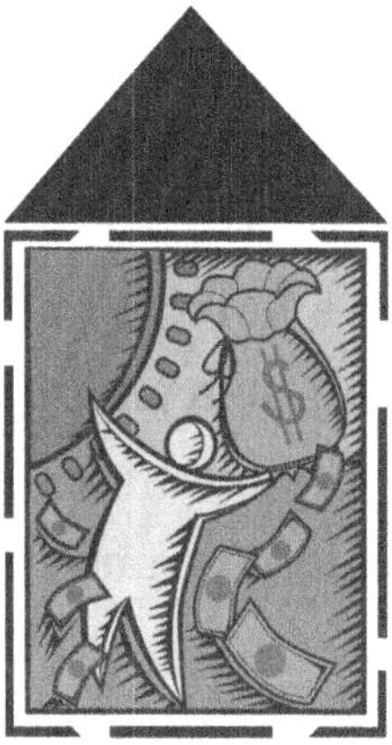

CHAPTER 2

Residential vs. Commercial Property Equity: Is There a Difference?

In this chapter you will:

- Learn the similarities between residential and commercial properties
- Learn the differences between residential and commercial properties
- Understand how these differences affect equity buildup in the various types of property

There are similarities in financing residential and commercial real estate properties, but there are also quite a few differences. These differences hold true when it comes to accessing the equity in the property as well.

Differences in Residential and Commercial Financing

The differences that exist between commercial and residential properties are based solely on the risk factor. Mortgage lenders consider commercial properties to be riskier investments than residential properties because if someone has to choose between paying for thc home they live in and a commercial property, the private property usually wins. Also, commercial properties tend to be for business purposes, and when businesses fail, commercial property payments cannot be met. Because commercial properties have a higher risk of default, lenders have different terms and conditions for the financing options available to commercial property buyers and owners.

While commercial properties are zoned for business use, residential properties are zoned for personal living use only, and the type of zoning indicates what type of financing a borrower can obtain on the property. If it is zoned commercially, then the property requires a commercial mortgage, which means higher interest rates and different qualification terms than that of a property zoned residentially. There are also different loan-to-value ratios for residential versus commercial properties. Typically, a lender will loan a lower percentage of the market value on a commercial property than it will on a residential property. These differences are all because of the risk associated with a commercial property being higher than that associated with a residential property. It comes down to the fact that residential properties tend to be a priority for borrowers to pay on and maintain because is it their haven, where they live, and where their family lives. If borrowers have to choose between paying on a mortgage for the property where they live and a property where they work, for instance, the residential property usually takes priority.

There are a variety of commercial property types, but some of the more common types include:

- Rental apartments or apartment complexes where there are five units or more
- Commercial rentals such office suite complexes, warehouse/office condo combos, office buildings
- Condo hotels (Condotels)
- Hotels and motels
- Industrial buildings
- Shopping centers
- Retail strip malls
- Office buildings
- Timeshares (not the individual units but the entire property)

Residential property types are more commonly understood than commercial property types. The basic definition of a residential property is a domicile or where someone lives. Some of the common types of residential properties include:

- Single-family homes
- Individual condominium units
- Individual apartment units
- Duplexes
- Apartment complexes up to four units
- Co-ops
- Townhouses

Risk factor

The risk factor for commercial properties affects all of the terms and conditions for financing and pulling equity out of the property. This includes the required down payment, the maximum amount that financing allows, the interest rate charged, and the length of the mortgage or equity line.

The down payment that most commercial lenders require is a greater percentage of the purchase price than that for the purchase of a residential property. The more money you put down on a property, the greater the amount of equity that exists in the property. For example, Bob buys a commercial property that costs $1 million. He is required to put a 30 percent down payment, which means he is financing $700,000. Bob then buys a $1 million home. He is required by the lender to put a 20 percent down payment, which means he is financing the balance of $800,000. Even though the purchase price for the commercial and residential property is the same, the equity in the property is different based on the down payment required: Bob has $300,000 of equity in his commercial property and $200,000 in his home.

Purchase price - Mortgage balance = Equity amount
Commercial property: $1,000,000 - $700,000 = $300,000
Residential property: $1,000,000 - $800,000 = $200,000

This illustrates how commercial properties can have more equity than residential properties based on the down payment amount required and the maximum financing amounts offered by lenders. Because commercial properties are used for business purposes, these types of properties tend to be less of a priority than a borrower's residential property. So if a borrower's business fails and he or she has to choose between making mortgage payment on his or her home and making the mortgage payment for his or her business, the mortgage payment on the home is probably going to be the priority.

This, combined with the fact that commercial properties generally cost more than residential ones, means there tends to be higher amounts of equity available in commercial properties. For example, Cody buys a primary residence for $250,000 and decides to put 30 percent down on the property. He also purchases a $500,000 warehouse for his business. He is required by the lender to put a 30 percent down payment on the property, and they will finance the other 70 percent. This means Cody has approximately $75,000 of equity in his home and $150,000 of equity in his warehouse.

Purchase price X Down payment percent = Equity amount
Commercial property: $150,000 X 0.30 = $150,000
Residential property: $250,000 X 0.30 = $75,000

Interest rates

The second major difference between financing and tapping equity in commercial and residential properties is the interest rate charged and the term of the mortgage. Commercial properties tend to have higher financing interest rates and shorter terms than residential mortgages do. While residential mortgage terms extend up to 30 years, commercial mortgage terms can be as short as five or ten years and typically extend to lengths of only 15 years. There are exceptions to this, where some commercial lenders offer terms that extend to 20 years. The shorter terms of commercial mortgages also affect the rate at which equity builds in the property. Because you have to pay off a commercial mortgage more quickly than a residential mortgage, commercial properties tend to build equity at a quicker rate than residential loans.

As for the interest rate differential, while a commercial mortgages typically runs anywhere from 5 to 8 percent more than the interest rates for a residential property. So if a residential mortgage is going for 6.5 percent, then a commercial mortgage may be going for 11.5 to 14.5 percent.

Qualification process

Qualifying for financing on a commercial property is completely different from qualifying for financing on a residential property. A commercial property financing qualification is dependent on the cash flow of the property combined with the property value itself. Some commercial lenders also require the individuals who own the commercial property – even if it is being financed under the company name – to qualify for the loan as well. This means that the owners are personally guaranteeing the loan, so if they default on the commercial loan, it is not only the business that is responsible — the individuals who guaranteed the loan are also responsible for the repayment. This requires tax returns, paystubs, and credit checks for those involved in establishing the financing for a commercial property.

A commercial property can have cash flow in a couple of different ways. If the property is being rented out to tenants, then the property obtains cash flow from the rent payments. In order to determine the cash flow, the expenses for operating the property are deducted from the income. There is another way a business can show cash flow for qualification purposes: For the business that is operating in the commercial property, it must show sufficient income to qualify for the loan. What is considered sufficient income depends on the amount of the loan and the guidelines sets forth by the lending institution.

A residential property that is your primary residence or vacation home does not have cash flow, so qualifying depends on your personal financial situation (your personal cash flow) in combination with the value of the property. In this case, your credit report and credit score are pulled; pay stubs and confirmation of employment are required; and your income and debts are all taken into consideration to see if you qualify for financing. It is important to keep in mind that your credit report contains your credit history, which are accounts you have with various creditors and your payment history with each of these creditors. Your credit score is directly related to your credit history, so if your credit history is good, then your score will be higher; if your credit score is below par, your score will be lower. Lenders will pull both your credit report and your credit score from each of the three credit reporting agencies to use for making a lending decision.

While the qualification process for commercial property financing does not have a direct effect on the equity in a commercial property, it does have an indirect effect because cash flow can be a determining factor in the amount of mortgage you can qualify for, which in turn affects the amount of equity in your property. The lower the amount of financing, the more money that is required in cash as a down payment. The higher the cash down payment, the higher the amount of equity built into the property. This is an indirect effect on the amount of equity because the lower the amount of financing you qualify for, the more of a down payment you will be required to put down. The higher your down payment, the more equity you have in the property right from the start, before taking into account any additional principal reduction payments or market value increases.

Investment vs. Commercial Properties

Newer real estate investors often confuse the terms investment property and commercial property. They think of an investment as anything they invest their money in to obtain a return on their investment, no matter how the property is zoned. Though buying a commercial property (or any real estate) can be seen as an investment, there is a difference in how the lender views the property, how the equity builds in the property, and how you can access the equity. Lenders across the United States consider an investment property as a property that is not your primary residence or second home; it is a property that is zoned residentially and contains one to four units that you lease to tenants. This means you may own a single-family home, a duplex, or three- or four-unit homes, where all of the units are rented out or available to be rented out to tenants. Even if you own these properties and they are not rented out, if it is not your primary residence or vacation home, it is considered an investment property.

Investment properties are similar to commercial properties when it comes to the fact that lenders view them as riskier investments. This causes lenders to require larger down payments on investment properties than they do for primary or vacation homes. Lenders also charge a higher interest rate for financing investment properties. The rates and terms for residential investment properties are more attractive than commercial property rates and terms. Because investment properties require more of a cash down payment, this means that your equity builds in the property faster than a residential property that does not require as much of a down payment.

There is also a distinction between owner-occupied commercial properties and commercial properties that are rented out or leased to tenants. Owner-occupied commercial properties are owned and occupied by the business or business owner; they have higher loan-to-value ratios than commercial properties that are leased or rented to other businesses or business owners, which means that the lender will finance a higher amount on owner-occupied properties versus rented or leased properties. This also means that owner-occupied units may start off with less equity than a leased commercial property because the lender requires less of a down payment.

It is important to remember that the more money you put down a property as a cash down payment, the more equity you have invested in the property. Is it always wise to put more money down and finance less to purchase or refinance a property, or is it better to use this cash for other purposes? It depends.

Every financial situation is different. You have to take a long, hard look at all of your options and then educate yourself on the options available. *Chapter 3 of this book goes into full detail on all of the ways that you can pull out the equity you have built up in your property and use it for other purposes.* Once you read the rest of this book, you should have a full understanding on the options that are available for you to access real estate equity and what you can invest this money into to earn a greater return than it will sitting in the home. Only when you have a full understanding can you truly determine whether you should build up equity quickly by putting more money down and making extra payments on your mortgage throughout the year, or redirect those funds into something that brings you a greater return on your investment than the real estate itself. This book is not solely about whether to put more money down or not; it is about what to do with the money that you already have in equity. Throughout the book, you will find information on the different ways that equity builds in real estate; ways that you can accelerate the equity buildup; how you can access this equity; and what you can invest your equity in to profit from your investment.

As you read through the book, remember that your goal in building up equity is to access this equity for better purposes than the sunk cost of sitting in real estate — or what some see as sitting on a pile of money. This is not to say that your investment in owning real estate is not a valuable investment, because it certainly can be. The point is that you can use your real estate investment as leverage to gain more, earn more, and create a better future for you, your business, and your family. So now that you know what equity is and how it builds, it is time to discover all of ways you can access that equity.

Checklist	
✓	Decide which type of property you are using to tap into your equity (Commercial property or residential property? How is it zoned?)
✓	Find lenders that offer equity financing options for your property type
✓	Make a list of how much equity you want to access from each property you are considering
✓	Decide on the possible use(s) for the equity funds once you have them
✓	Begin to compile this information so you can use it to access the equity after you finish reading the book
✓	Be sure to gather information from at least three lenders to compare and determine which lender offers the option most beneficial for your situation

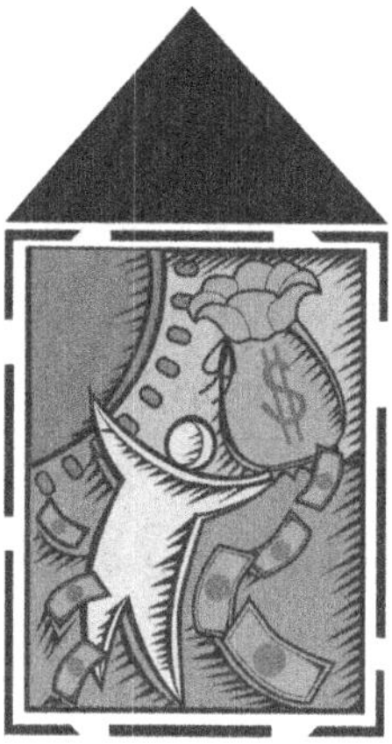

CHAPTER 3

Options for Tapping Your Equity

In this chapter you will:

- Learn the financing options available for accessing the equity in your property
- Discover how these financing options may differ between residential and commercial properties
- Understand how a home equity line of credit differs from a home equity loan
- Learn how home equity lines and loans compare to pulling out the equity with a mortgage
- Uncover the reasons why one financing option may be better than another for your personal financial situation
- Determine the financing option that is the best for you to pull equity out of your property

You learned earlier that the amount of potential equity you have in your home can be determined by taking the amount you owe on the property from the value of the property. Maybe you have been adding extra to your mortgage payments to pay off your mortgage early, which is also helping you to build equity in the property. Maybe the property value has increased since you originally bought it. Whatever the reason, you have equity sitting in your real estate property, and you want to know your options for getting it out. This is also referred to as tapping into or accessing your equity. In essence, when you are accessing the equity in your home, you are using your home as collateral in order to secure a loan with the bank or mortgage lender.

There are quite a few financing options available for doing this. There are different factors that go into determining which option is the right one for your situation. Two of the main factors that play a role in the decision are what you are going to use the funds for and how you need to access the funds. When you have an immediate need for the funds, then it is typically better to use a home equity loan. With a home equity loan, there are closing costs involved in establishing it, and you receive the equity monies in a lump sum payment, but the interest rate is typically lower (1 to 2 percentage points) than a home equity line of credit.

When you do not have an immediate need for the funds and you need to access the funds a little bit at a time, or you are simply establishing a line for emergency purposes, then an equity line of credit is usually preferred. While the interest rate on an equity line is typically 1 to 2 percentage points higher than a home equity loan, it does not usually have closing costs associated with it, and you can access the funds using convenience checks or a debit card as you need it, rather than all at once. Because you can access the funds little by little, you are only paying interest on the amount of money that you have used. In essence, if you set up the line of credit but never use it, then you will not be charged any interest on it. With a home equity loan, however, you have to take the full amount at once, and you are charged interest on it right away, whether you use the funds right away or not.

Home Equity Line of Credit (HELOC)

One of the most popular ways to access the equity in your property is with a home equity line of credit, which is also referred to as a HELOC. Typically, a home equity line of credit is placed as second lien position on your property — taking a backseat to your first mortgage. If you do not have a first mortgage, and you own your property free and clear, then the home equity line of credit would be considered your first lien. The lien position is simply the order the creditors are paid if something were to happen and the property is foreclosed on.

HELOCs work a lot like credit cards because they are revolving lines of credit. When you open a home equity line of credit, you are provided with checks — some lenders provide a debit or credit card — that allow you to access the funds. You are only charged interest on the balance you use on the account, so if you never access the line, then you are not required to make monthly payments. Generally, lenders do not charge a penalty or any additional fees for setting up an equity line that is never used. When you do access the line or have an unpaid balance on the equity line, then you are charged interest, which is calculated on the outstanding balance. When you pay down the balance or pay off the balance you owe, the line is available for you to use over again. You can easily see how this operates similarly to a consumer credit card.

Many lenders do not charge fees or closing costs to establish a HELOC, which is why many homeowners set up an equity line in case they need to access these funds for an emergency. Other lenders charge minor setup fees that equate to a couple of hundred dollars or less. HELOC interest rates run higher than first mortgages, but are lower than credit card and consumer loan interest rates. HELOC interest payments are generally tax deductible, so it is a less expensive route to take than using a credit card or consumer loan to make a purchase. HELOC interest rates tend to be based on the prime rate plus a margin, which is the amount added to the current prime rate; this figures out the interest rate on the HELOC that is used to calculate your monthly payment due. For example, if the current prime rate is 4.75 percent and the margin for your HELOC is 2 percent, then the interest rate on your HELOC is 6.75 percent. The margin may vary according to the lender, how much of a credit line you have established, and your credit score. The less risk the lender is taking by extending a line of credit to you, the lower your margin may be. So if you have a high credit score (typically 720 or higher), you are more likely to receive more favorable terms (a lower margin results in a lower interest rate) than borrowers with poor credit.

Home Equity Loan

Similar to a home equity line of credit, home equity loans also allow you to tap into the equity you have in property, but a home equity loan is not a revolving line of credit, so it is funded in a lump sum. This means that you start accruing interest on it at the time of closing, whether you use the money or not. As you pay down or pay off a home equity loan, it is not available for you to use again. If you want to tap into your equity after the loan is paid off, you have to take out a new equity loan. Interest rates on home equity loans are still higher than first mortgages, but lower than credit cards and consumer loans. Typically, the interest rate for a home equity line of credit is lower than a home equity loan because a home equity loan is less risky, as funds are received as a lump sum. This is because the lender knows how much the equity balance is and how much of a payment they expect to receive each month. Because equity lines of credit can be accessed as needed (in amounts up to the maximum), the lender does not know how much may be outstanding on your equity line at any given time. To give you an idea of how the interest rates between a home equity line of credit and a home equity loan vary, as of September 10, 2009, the national average for a home equity line of credit is 5.88 percent, while a home equity loan is 8.03 percent, according to BankRate.com.

It is important to note that interest rates can and do change daily — sometimes more than once in the same day. Lenders set interest rates based on what is happening in the bond market and the mortgage-backed securities (MBS) market. While there are several complicated, behind-the-scenes factors that mortgage analysts and professional working for the lenders use to calculate what interest rates will be charged to mortgage borrowers, you only need to be aware of one thing: Interest rates typically move in the opposite direction of the bond market, so as bond values increase, mortgage rates tend to decrease. When bond values decrease, mortgage rates tend to increase.

Home equity loans typically have closing costs associated with establishing them. The closing costs may be lower than a first mortgage, but they are more involved in establishing a home equity line of credit. So, why choose one over the other?

The answer is rather straightforward because it is a matter of simple math. First, it depends on what your intentions are — the use(s) for the money — and how and when you need to access it. If you have an immediate need for the entire amount of the money, then it is usually beneficial to take it in a lump sum in the form of a home equity loan. Although there are costs involved in setting up a home equity loan, the lower interest rate usually causes you to break even quicker than a home equity line of credit.

If you need to access the money little by little rather than all at once, then a HELOC is usually the better option because you can access it when you need it and are only charged on what you use. For example, if you are paying for your child's college education, you need enough money to pay for tuition, room and board, and books over four years. With an equity line, you can make each of these small payments when they come due, and you will only be responsible for paying interest on the outstanding balance. You will pay less over time than if you receive the money in a lump sum, where you start paying interest on the money right away even if you have not used it.

One example when a home equity loan may be more beneficial than a home equity line of credit is when you are using the loan to consolidate debt. Because you will be using the money you receive from the home equity loan right away to pay off all of your old debts to consolidate them into one loan, you will benefit from the lower interest rate that home equity loans provide over home equity lines of credit.

In Chapter 5 of this book, we will talk in detail about your options for investing the home equity funds you tap into. The investment vehicles you choose may also help you to determine which of these two options is the most beneficial for you. But your options do not end with home equity lines of credit and home equity loans. There are still other ways you can access the equity in your property.

Cash-out Refinancing with Mortgages

You also have the option of doing a cash-out refinance, which is when you refinance your first mortgage and pull equity out of the property simultaneously. When you do a cash-out refinance, you establish a new first mortgage for the amount of the original mortgage, plus the additional cash you receive from accessing your equity. You will receive the equity amount in the form of a check when you close on the new mortgage. Similar to a home equity loan, you are now responsible for paying interest on the whole new amount of the mortgage. It is not a revolving line of credit; it is a regular mortgage and acts as such. This means that it is established as a new mortgage in first lien position on the home. When you refinance, you are paying off your old existing mortgage balance and establishing a new loan for the full amount of your original mortgage, plus the cash you pulled out of the home. As you would with any first mortgage, this means that you are required to make monthly principal and interest payments based on the new loan balance.

The two main advantages of choosing a cash-out refinance over a HELOC or home equity loan are the interest rate and the term for repayment. The interest rate on a standard first lien position mortgage is usually lower than what would be considered a second loan. The term on a first mortgage is typically longer than equity lines or loans, so you have a longer timeframe to repay the mortgage. As of September 2009, the national average for a 30-year-fixed-rate mortgage is approximately 5 percent, and the national average for a home equity line is approximately 8 percent, according to BankRate.com Again, there are closing costs that have to be paid when doing a cash-out refinance, but with the lower interest rate, the break-even point is usually faster than that of a home equity loan. Generally, the break-even point on a cash-out refinance is approximately four years, while it can be almost double (approximately eight years) to break-even on a home equity loan.

When you decide to do a cash-out refinance as your option for taking equity out of your property, the mortgage options available to you are the same as if you were purchasing or refinancing without taking money out. Your options for cash-out refinancing include fixed-rate mortgages, adjustable-rate mortgages, fixed-to-adjustable-rate mortgages, interest-only mortgages, and piggybacking. Balloon mortgages are another option, although it is more common to use balloon mortgages with commercial properties rather than residential.

Cash-out refinances are typically used when borrowers want to tap into the equity in their home and can receive a lower interest rate than they are currently paying on their mortgage. This might be because interest rates have dropped since the initial mortgage was established, or the credit score of the borrowers has increased since the original mortgage was established. Typically, the lowest interest rates and more favorable loan terms go to borrowers with higher credit scores rather than borrowers with low credit scores. Furthermore, the lending market collapse has tightened loan qualifications, raising the minimum credit score to 620 to be approved for a mortgage loan. It is often used even when the blended rate — the rate on the new first mortgage and the equity line or loan — is less than or comparable to the current rate being paid on the first mortgage (also taking into consideration that a higher loan amount is now being financed).

Fixed-rate mortgages

Probably one of the most popular and most commonly used mortgages is the good old-fashioned fixed-rate mortgage. Fixed-rate mortgages typically come in 15- and 30-year terms, but some lenders offer 20- and 25-year options. There are a few lenders that offer mortgage terms that extend out to 40 years, but this is extremely rare. Especially during the 2007 to 2009 recession, when the housing and mortgage industries were struggling with the economic hard time, lenders wanted to reduce their risk of borrower foreclosures or overextending credit. This meant that the lenders were less willing to loan long-term but would rather reduce their risk by with short-term lending. More common terms are the 15- and 30-year terms. These types of mortgages provide the borrowers who use them peace of mind because the interest rate and the monthly mortgage payment never change. Borrowers also know that their mortgages will be paid off during the term of the loan if they do not choose to make extra payments or pay it off early. The main disadvantage of these long-term loans is that the borrower tends to pay more in interest than if the term of the loan was shorter.

For example, if you are buying a home but are very conservative or live on a fixed income, then a fixed-rate mortgage may be the best option for you. The fixed-rate option may provide you with peace of mind so that you know what your monthly payment is every month for the rest of the time that you live in the home. The downside of a fixed-rate, long-term mortgage is that you tend to pay more in interest overall than you would have paid with a short-term mortgage.

If you take out a mortgage for $150,000 and want to compare what you would pay in total using a 15-year fixed-rate mortgage to a 30-year fixed-rate mortgage, you can use an amortization schedule calculator to find the result. Using the amortization calculator on BankRate.com (**www.bankrate.com/calculators/mortgages/amortization-calculator.aspx**), you would end up paying a total amount of interest of $209,263.35 at the end of a 30-year loan, while you would pay total interest of $92,683.63 at the end of a 15-year loan. You would save over $116,000 by having a 15-year mortgage rather than a 30-year mortgage ($209,263.35 - $92.683.63 = $116,579.72).

Adjustable-rate mortgages

As the name implies, adjustable-rate mortgages do not have a fixed interest rate, so as the interest rate changes, so does the monthly mortgage payment. This can be advantageous if interest rates are dropping, but can be a disadvantage if interest rates are rising. Because the future is unknown, some borrowers do not feel comfortable not knowing what their interest rate and monthly payments will be. Some adjustable-rate mortgages adjust monthly, while others change every six months or once a year.

So, what makes an interest rate change? It is typically the state of the economy that drives whether interest rates rise or fall, so it is important to understand what affects your mortgage interest rate if you have an adjustable-rate mortgage. One of the main ways interest rates are affected is by the bond market and the actions taken by the Federal Reserve. For example, in 2008 and 2009, the Federal Reserve continued to cut interest rates in an effort to stimulate the failing economy. With lower interest rates, the Federal Reserve encourages borrowers to borrow because lower interest rates mean more affordable payments; in turn, this stimulates the economy. As the economy stabilizes, the Federal Reserve may increase interest rates, which typically slows down the amount of borrowing and lending taking place.

The closing costs are the same as those associated with establishing a fixed-rate mortgage. The difference comes in the interest rate. Adjustable-rate mortgages have interest rates that are generally lower than fixed-rate mortgages, so they help those looking for a lower monthly payment than the one they can get from a fixed-rate mortgage. This, of course, can change if interest rates suddenly spike or increase over the term of the mortgage. Because of the lower interest rate and lower monthly mortgage payments, it is typically easier for borrowers to qualify for an adjustable-rate mortgage than it is for a fixed-rate mortgage.

Think about it logically. A lower interest rate is going to provide a lower monthly mortgage payment. When a mortgage lender is qualifying you for a mortgage, they not only take your existing expenses into consideration, but they also consider your monthly mortgage payment. A lower mortgage payment is going to keep the qualifying rations lenders use to approve you for a loan lower, which equates to being less of a risk for the lender than someone with higher ratios. A fixed-rate mortgage that typically has a higher interest rate than adjustable-rate mortgages brings higher monthly mortgage payments, which throws your qualifying ratios higher and may make your ratios too high to get approval on the loan.

For example, if you buy a home today but expect the interest rates to decrease over the next three years that you plan on living in the home, then an adjustable-rate mortgage may be the right mortgage option for you. Although there is no guarantee on what will happen with interest rates in the future, you have an expectation that interest rates will increase – maybe the Federal Reserve has been meeting and hinting at the fact that they intend to drop rates – so if and when the interest rates do drop, you will benefit by paying a lower mortgage rate when your rate adjusts. The downside of this is if the rates go up instead of down, you will be paying a higher interest rate and monthly mortgage payment than you were when you first established the mortgage.

Fixed-to-adjustable-rate mortgages

As it sounds, fixed-to-adjustable-rate mortgages have characteristics that combine fixed-rate and adjustable-rate mortgages. These types of mortgages have a fixed interest rate for a specified period of time, then adjust after the fixed rate period has expired.

Terms for fixed-to-adjustable-rate mortgages vary by lender, but common fixed-rate terms are five, seven, and ten years. Overall, these are 30-year mortgages, so the remaining 25, 23, and 20 years, respectively, are the terms for the adjustable rate period. These fixed-to-adjustable-rate mortgages can be beneficial when you know that you will only live in or own the property for a certain period of time. It provides a fixed interest rate (which is generally lower than fixed-rate mortgages) and constant monthly payments for the fixed-rate period. Closing costs for fixed-to-adjustable-rate mortgages are calculated the same as they are for fixed-rate mortgages, but qualifying for these mortgages tends to be easier than a 15- or 30-year fixed-rate mortgage because of the lower interest rate and monthly payment.

The main disadvantage of these types of mortgages is that your interest rate can go up or down, which also causes your monthly payment to go up and down. This means that you may not know from one month to the next – or one year to the next – what your mortgage payment will be. While a decrease in payments is not typically seen as a disadvantage, an increase in payments can be. Payments that increase at too much of a drastic rate can create a situation where you can no longer afford to make your mortgage payment. Not being able to make your mortgage payment can lead you to default on your mortgage, which can ultimately lead to foreclosure.

For example, if you buy a home to live in for the next five years, and then you plan to retire in a different state, a five-year, fixed-to-adjustable-rate mortgage may be the perfect solution for you. You will enjoy a lower rate and mortgage payment than a 15- or 30-year fixed rate, and because you are selling the property in five years, it will not matter to you that the mortgage adjusts after the fifth year.

There is no doubt why these types of mortgages were created or became wildly popular in the last decade or so. The national average states that Americans move every five to seven years. If they do not move, then they refinance during this same time frame. Gone are the days when your parents or grandparents had the same mortgage for 25 or 30 years. Gone are the days where we live in our homes for 25 or 30 years; thus, flexible mortgage options such as these were created to better fit the needs of the modern American borrower.

Interest-only mortgages

Interest-only mortgages tend to have terms that are similar to fixed-to-adjustable-rate mortgages. These mortgages usually come with fixed rate terms of five, seven, or ten years. The period is also the time when interest-only payments are required. Overall, interest-only mortgages tend to be 30-year mortgages, so after the fixed rate and interest-only period, it fully amortizes for the remaining 25, 23, or 20 years, respectively. These mortgages use a simple interest calculation to determine the monthly interest payment. As an easy example, if your mortgage is $100,000 at an interest rate of 7 percent, your interest payment is calculated with the following formula:

Mortgage balance X Interest rate / Months in a year = Mortgage interest payment
$100,000 X 0.07 / 12 = $583.33

This is the minimum payment due every month. Because it only includes interest, nothing is applied to reduce the principal balance of the mortgage. So, if you make the interest-only payment, then when the mortgage fully amortizes, the original mortgage balance is used to calculate the principal and interest payments now due. If, however, you choose to pay more than the minimum, the difference is applied to the principal balance of the mortgage. *This type of mortgage was illustrated as an option for accelerating the equity buildup in your property in Chapter 2.* Many borrowers, however, choose to only pay the interest.

Why? Everyone has their reasons, but savvy investors realize that their money is better spent elsewhere, rather than sinking their funds into real estate. This was especially true when it is a bull market — when the stock market is climbing, and you can earn a greater return on investing your money in an investment vehicle that pays more than a piece of real estate that is probably only going to appreciate 1-2 percent per year.

For example, if you intend on owning a home for only a few years and do not have any interest in building equity in the home, an interest-only mortgage keeps your monthly mortgage payments low (because it does not include principal), and you can generally deduct the entire interest portion of your mortgage on your taxes. This excludes people in certain tax brackets and for mortgage amounts over a certain limit, so check with your tax advisor to make sure an interest-only mortgage is a viable option for your financial situation.

In the end, no matter what type of mortgage you choose, you always have the option to make additional payments to reduce the principal. One pitfall you need to be aware of with interest-only mortgages is that some involve negative amortization, which occurs when the monthly payment is not enough to cover the full amount of interest. This causes the insufficient amount to be added to the principal balance of the mortgage, causing your principal balance to increase rather than stay the same (if you are paying enough to cover the interest). If the lender is not using a simple interest calculation or is requiring an amount less than the interest portion, the loan has negative amortization. Negative amortization can take place on any type of mortgage, but it seems to be prevalent in interest-only mortgages. If you are investigating an interest-only loan, be sure to ask if the loan has negative amortization.

Balloon mortgages

Balloon mortgages are financing options typically available for commercial properties, but there are lenders that offer these types of mortgages for residential financing as well. A balloon mortgage is a short-term financing option; common terms are five and seven years. At the end of the term, a balloon payment comes due, so you either have to pay the balance of the mortgage or refinance it to establish a new mortgage. These types of mortgages mimic fixed-rate mortgages but also have some features of interest-only mortgages.

Similar to a fixed-rate mortgage, monthly mortgage payments for a balloon mortgage are fixed, so borrowers do enjoy a level payment for the term of the mortgage. The difference between a fixed-rate mortgage and a balloon mortgage is that the monthly payments are not amortized, so the mortgage is not paid-in-full by the end of the term. This means at the end of the term, there is still a principal balance due. This is the time when the mortgage either has to be paid off or refinanced.

Some lenders also offer conversion options for balloon mortgages. These vary by lender but may entail the balloon mortgage automatically converting to a 30-year, fixed-rate mortgage at a higher interest rate than the balloon mortgage interest rate. These conversion terms are established at the onset of the loan, so it will state the margin that is added to your current rate or the index used to calculate the new mortgage interest rate (the converted mortgage interest rate). These conversion rates usually offer interest rates that are higher than the market, so it is usually more beneficial to refinance a balloon mortgage rather than convert.

Piggybacking

Piggybacking is an industry term used when you establish a first mortgage and a second mortgage (usually an equity line of credit or home equity loan) at the same time. Many borrowers use piggybacking when purchasing a property in order to finance a higher amount, so they have to come up with less of a down payment. It is also a great way to tap into your equity when purchasing or refinancing a property. This type of loan is sometimes called an 80/20 loan because while you are financing 100 percent of the purchase price, the lender finances 80 percent of the price with a first mortgage and the remaining 20 percent as a HELOC or a home equity loan. If the second loan is a home equity line, then as you pay down the balance, it is available for you to use again.

The process for establishing a piggyback loan is seamless to the borrower. There may be a small fee charged by the lender to establish the two loans instead of one loan. Other lenders charge closing costs based on the full amount (sum of the first and second mortgage), depending on whether it is a line of credit or equity loan in second position. The borrower, however, attends one closing for both mortgages.

When you use a piggyback loan, your first mortgage choices are typically the same, so you can choose a fixed-rate, adjustable-rate, or fixed-to-adjustable-rate mortgage. Your second mortgage options are a home equity line of credit or home equity loan. Depending on the lender, you may not have a choice on the type of the second mortgage; they may choose it for you. How you should go about choosing the option that is right for you is covered in the rest of this chapter.

Determining the Financing Option Right for You

Having all these options available to you may seem daunting. It is similar to going to a restaurant whose menu has pages and pages of food choices. It makes it hard to decide which one is right for you or which one you want. Because every financial situation is different, it is difficult to write blanket statements that encompass every scenario, so it is up to you to take the information provided and apply it to your own personal financial situation and your goals.

Your first step should be to find out which options are available to you. The above-mentioned options are the general categories but may not be available with the lender you work with, or may not be available to you because of your credit, income, or other situation. For example, if you have bad credit, you may have to work with a lender that caters to bad-credit borrowers, which means your interest rate is probably going to be higher than a good-credit borrower, and the mortgage options may be limited to an adjustable-rate or fixed-to-adjustable-rate mortgage.

On the flip side, even if you have good credit, there may be other factors, such as the amount of outstanding debt you have, that limit you to certain types of mortgages. For example, a mortgage lender runs a debt-to-income ratio in order to see if you fall with the lender's guidelines. If you have a debt-to-income ratio that is higher than the lender's guidelines — because you have a large amount of debt that is eating up the majority of your income — then the lender may approve you for a mortgage but require that you use a specific type of mortgage, such as an adjustable-rate mortgage. Because adjustable-rate mortgages tend to have lower interest rates than fixed-rate mortgages, adjustable-rate mortgage payments are generally lower, too. With a lower mortgage payment, your debt-to-income ratio is kept from going as high as it would with the higher mortgage payment that a fixed-rate mortgage may bring.

Once you know which financing options are available, you then need to find out all of the costs and terms associated with the mortgages. This includes any upfront costs such as application fees, closing costs, monthly payments, interest rates, and the terms or length of the mortgages. These factors may dictate which option is the best one for you as well. Closing costs can vary from lender to lender, so it is a good idea to compare at least three lenders before making a final decision on which one is offering the most financially beneficial program for you. Closing costs do not tend to vary according to your credit score or personal financial situation, but lenders do want to see that you have enough money in cash (in bank accounts or cash equivalent accounts such as stocks and bonds that can be liquidated) to cover the closing costs. In a refinance situation, you may have the option of rolling the closing costs into the amount of the mortgage loan so that you do not have to pay the closing costs out of your pocket.

Your final step in determining which option is the most beneficial to you really depends on what you intend to do with the equity you are pulling out of the property. If you use the money to buy another piece of real estate, invest in a stock portfolio, or put in a mutual fund to pay for a child's college education, the potential return on the investment is the main factor in deciding which financing option and investment vehicle combination creates the best scenario for you.

After you read the rest of this book, revisit the financing option section again. After you learn more about what you can invest your equity in, you will be better versed on how you can use your equity today to invest for tomorrow. This is the best way to determine which financing option benefits you the most in the long run.

Checklist	
✓	Using the list of lenders you made at the end of Chapter 2, determine which financing options are available to you with these lenders
✓	Determine other factors, such as credit, credit score, or income, that may limit your financing options
✓	Inquire for any further information you need from these lenders on financing options available to you
✓	Read the terms, conditions, and interest rates for each lender
✓	Familiarize yourself with each lender, their mortgage process, and their requirements to get a feel for which lender may be the best fit for you
✓	If you do not understand, ask questions

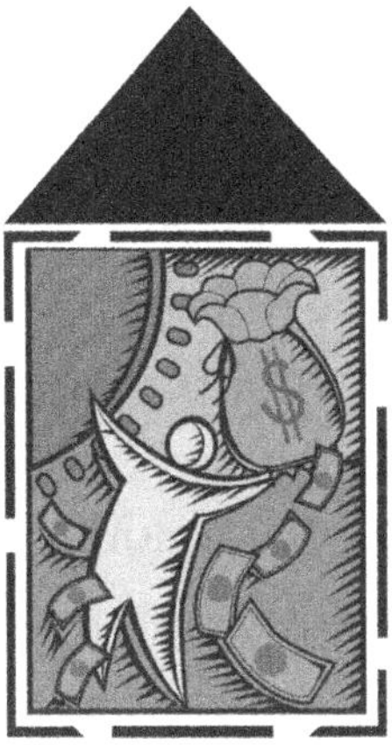

CHAPTER 4

Determining the Equity in Your Property

In this chapter you will:

- Learn how to figure out how much equity you have in your property
- See how the equity amount differs in residential and commercial properties
- Gain a full understanding of how lenders figure the amount of equity in a property
- Find out what seasoning requirements are and how this may affect your ability to tap the equity in a property

In the first chapter we discussed the simple calculation for determining how much equity you have in your property — subtracting the mortgage balance from the estimated value of the property. Unfortunately, this is not how mortgage lenders calculate how much equity they will allow you to access on the property because the more they loan, the higher the risk is to the lender. Equity access calculations vary by lender. It even varies by the type of financing you use to tap into the equity. To complicate matters further, the percentage also varies by the type of property. Primary residences, for example, have a higher percentage than second homes, investment properties, and commercial properties. This chapter simplifies the process so you have an idea of how much money you may be able to get from the equity in your property.

Before you approach a lender, you can estimate the amount of equity you have in your home or commercial property. This helps you decide if exploring the option of pulling out money is available to you. Otherwise you may waste a lot of time and energy searching for and talking with lenders only to find out that you do not have enough equity in your property to even access it for your needs. A mortgage lender or broker can help you determine the exact amount of equity available to you, but it requires going through the formal channels of applying for equity financing. This involves pulling your credit report, having an appraisal of the property completed, requesting current mortgage balances from your lender, ordering title work to be done on the property, and preparing the loan documents and promissory note to be filed with the local county clerk's office. During this process, the lender surveys comparable real estate properties sold in the area located in and around your property (a.k.a. comps). Comps are used to determine the market value of the property or what the property could currently sell for.

Rather than go through the formal process to then find out that you do not qualify or that there is not enough equity in your property, you can do an informal analysis on your own. Check the real estate section of your local newspaper or specialty publications that cover real estate for your area. These sections and publications include a listing of properties currently for sale and properties that recently sold in the circulation area. The listings may be separated by area such as county, zip code, or neighborhood. Look for the properties that are located closely (within 1-2 miles) to the street where your home or commercial building is located, as proximity is one major factor to look for because the market value of a property is determined by similarities in square footage and location. The second important factor is that the comps also have similar square footage, the same number of bedrooms, a garage (or no garage), and other amenities.

For example, if you find a listing for a home in your neighborhood that is equal in size — with the same number of bedrooms, bathrooms, and similar garage — that recently sold for $300,000, it is reasonable to expect your home to be the same in value. If you owe $150,000 on your home, then you can assume you have about $150,000 in equity accumulated. There are many factors that go into calculating the valuation of properties, but this exercise at least makes you aware that accessing the equity in your home is a possible option.

Residential Properties

A typical percentage used by lenders to determine the amount of equity available as an HELOC or a home equity loan is 85 percent of the primary residence's value, minus the balance of the first mortgage. So, if your home is worth $250,000 and you have a first mortgage of $100,000, then the amount of equity you can access from the property is $112,500.

(Home value X Loan percent of value) - Existing mortgage balance = Available equity
($250,000 X 0.85) - $100,000 = $112,500

Second homes have HELOC and home equity loan calculations of around 75 percent, and investment properties can be 50 percent or lower. Other lenders will not allow equity lines of credit or home equity loans on investment properties at all because it doubles the risk to lenders. Not only are investment properties riskier, but adding an equity line in second lien position on an investment property is an added risk most lenders are not willing to take because it increases the amount of money that they might lose if the property owner defaults on the loan.

Commercial Properties

Equity lines and loans are viable options for commercial properties, too, but equity and interest rate are calculated differently from residential properties. Loan to values — the percentage used for the calculation — is lower for commercial properties than it is for residential properties because commercial properties have higher risk. Though you may be able obtain 85 percent of the value of a residential property minus any liens on the property, commercial properties can usually obtain 50-70 percent of the value minus current mortgage balances. Interest rates for commercial property equity lines of credit and equity loans are typically higher than residential properties. Again, this goes back to the fact that commercial properties are higher risks to lenders than residential properties are.

Seasoning Requirement

Terms and conditions for mortgages, home equity lines of credit, and home equity loans vary by lender. You have seen this in the loan-to-value calculations, interest rates, the term of the mortgage, and the payment calculations. Some lenders also impose other terms and conditions as to when you can establish and pay off a mortgage, equity line, or equity loan.

Lenders can impose a prepayment penalty for loans paid off before the maturity date because they lose money if a borrower pays off the loan before it matures. Typical prepayment penalties only last for the first few years of the mortgage. These fees can equal 2 to 5 percent of the remaining balance of the mortgage, which can be hefty when you have a large mortgage balance. Make sure you read prepayment penalty terms of your mortgage before you establish it. This can affect your time frame for refinancing a mortgage or paying the mortgage off without incurring additional fees. Residential mortgages carry prepayment penalties, but it is more common in commercial mortgages.

Another term you should be familiar with is seasoning requirements. Lenders can impose a stipulation that prohibits a borrower from refinancing or establishing an equity line or loan on a property based on the number of years they have owned the property. Lenders that impose seasoning rights may do this because they feel it represents a premature inflated market value of the property. A seasoning requirement may state that you have to own a property for one year before the lender will allow you to refinance your existing mortgage with them. This is important because you may not be able to access the equity in your property right away; you may have to wait for the seasoning requirement to pass with the lender of your choice, or turn to a lender that does not have a seasoning requirement.

Checklist	
✓	Calculate the amount of estimated equity you have in your property
✓	Determine if this is enough equity for you to invest
✓	Continue to research lenders that you are interested in working with
✓	Narrow it down to the top three lenders you are interested in
✓	Determine if these lenders have any seasoning requirement
✓	If they do, determine if you have owned the property long enough to tap into the equity
✓	Obtain the financing options available to you, the interest rate, APR, closing costs, and fees associated with each option
✓	Using the information from this book and the information provided by the lender, choose the financing option that is best for your needs
✓	Request and complete the application process for the financing option of your choice

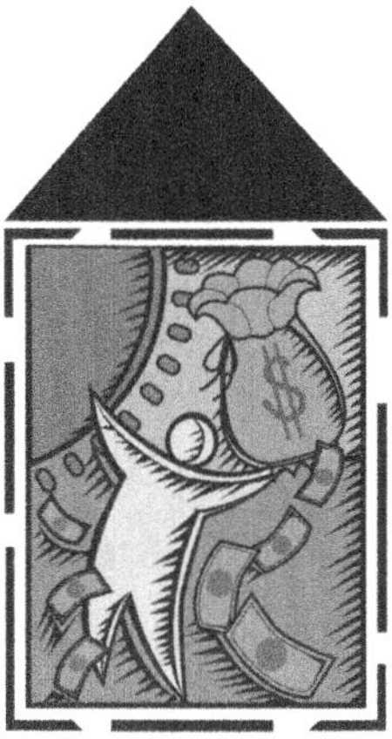

CHAPTER 5

You Have Tapped the Equity — Now What?

In this chapter you will:

- Discover the common ways equity funds are spent
- Receive an overview of some of the wiser options for investing your equity funds that gain you a greater return on your investment
- Determine how to assess the risk of your investment option before you use your equity funds
- Gain a full understanding of your investment risk factor
- Learn how diversification can increase your return on investment
- Learn the steps you need to take after you have set up your equity line, loan, or mortgage

Some homeowners and business owners across the U.S. are sitting on piles of cash in the real estate properties they own. Many do not even realize the amount of money they are sitting on because they do not understand what real estate equity is, how they can access it, and what they can do with the equity to earn the property owners more money than it is earning in the property. These are piles that could be put to good work if they tap into the equity in these properties. Equity in homes and commercial properties can be used to pay off debt, invest in other homes or businesses, and fund retirement or other types of investment accounts. Leveraging the equity in a property is all about putting your money to work for you. When you put your money to work for you, it is multiplying, 24 hours a day, seven days a week, making money even while you sleep.

Using the equity in your home or business property is not only for the rich. It is for smart individuals who know how to leverage the assets they have, using the tools that are available to them. In other words: Put what you have to work for you. As a homeowner or business owner with equity in that home or business, you have an opportunity to cash in that resource and use it today to invest for tomorrow.

There are various ways you can use the equity in your home or business to build a nest egg (funding a retirement account) or finance a specific purpose (paying for a child's college education) by investing your equity in additional real estate properties, buying a mutual fund, building a stock portfolio, or insuring investments you own. When you use the equity to fund an investment account for your retirement years, it provides you with a way to plan for your future. This is a great way to help ensure that you have enough money to live out your golden years in the lifestyle to which you are accustomed living. Investing in your own or your child's education can also be a lucrative and wise investment. An education can provide you or your child with a ticket to a higher-paying job or career opportunity, so it is an investment that more than pays for itself in the long run.

You can also invest your money back into your home or commercial property by updating your kitchen, refinishing the basement, or pulling up the carpet and refinishing the hardwood floors beneath it. These are all smart ways to invest your money because home improvements such as these allow you to build on the equity you already have amassed, and these types of home improvements can also increase the value of the property when you sell it. Exploring a new business idea or starting a new business is another lucrative option to getting a greater return on your investment than it is making by sitting in your home or property. You have costs involved in starting a business, but a business brings you short- and long-term income and a reasonable return on your investment.

The problem is that many homeowners and business owners who tap into their equity use it on frivolous purchases that are sunk costs that are gone forever once the money is spent — they will not see a return on that money — rather than investments that can earn them more money over time. People typically use their home or business equity to invest in declining assets such as cars, boats, and vacations. While it is nice to drive a luxurious car or boat, or spend time resting and relaxing on lavish and expensive vacations, once you spend this money it becomes a debt in the form of a home equity line, loan, or other mortgage you have used to access the equity in your home. It is not an investment by any means; once you spend the money on airline tickets, a hotel room, and expensive five-star restaurant meals, that money is gone forever — or, at least, until your mortgage or equity line bill comes the following month and you have to pay it, rather than having your money pay you.

Investing your equity today for tomorrow is not about taking unnecessary risks or about putting yourself in a position where you are living beyond your means. Equity in your home is not free money to gamble with, but instead it is the avenue you can take or the asset you can tap into that allows you to capitalize on the assets your home or commercial property represents. In essence, when you are using the equity in your home to make purchases or investments, you are using your home as collateral in order to secure a loan with the bank or mortgage lender. Capitalizing on your assets allow you to build upon the money you have. So before you pull the equity out of your home or business to make a purchase of any kind, stop and ask yourself how you are going to receive a return on your investment, or if it is going to put you in a better financial position in the future. If you can answer yes to the question, then it is an opportunity that you may want to take advantage of.

Measure Your Success

What you deem a success may not be a success to someone else, so it is important to set goals for yourself in regard to any of the investment options you choose. Writing down how you define success helps you save your time and money because it keeps you from making investment choices that will not allow you to reach your goal. In this case, success means using your equity funds to make more money and build a more stable financial future for you and your family. Before you use the equity in your real estate, make sure you are investing for the right reasons.

It is not about making your investment choices to keep up with friends, family members, or coworkers. It is about understanding the goals and possible outcomes of your investments. There is some form of risk involved in any and every investment option you choose. How great or low the risk depends on the option; whether you take the risk depends on you.

Take a moment to write down your definition of success. How will you measure the success of your investment? Is it about having the same tangible items as the people you view as successful? Is it about being able to retire early and having enough money to live the lifestyle you are accustomed to during your retirement? Is it about buying investment real estate properties whose rents become your monthly "paycheck?" The answers to the question "How do you measure success?" vary from person to person, but the various ways you can invest your money offer you the opportunity to reach your definition of true success.

Measure Your Risk

Conservative financial experts caution against using your equity to reinvest because they feel the investment is the real estate that is holding the equity. More liberal investors argue that the equity in a home or business property does little for you if you leave it sitting there. The equity in a property grows, but it does not tend to multiply in a manner that makes you feel your money is working for you; it does not tend to make your money grow as fast or as much as what is available with other investment vehicles. Having equity in real estate allows you to realize your dreams if you dare to reach high enough. Because you are pulling money out of your home, you want to use it wisely so it can be a springboard to opportunities you might not otherwise realize. However, whether you should take that big step out there is not always an easy decision.

According to financial consultant and contributor to the popular investment site **www.BankRate.com** Don Taylor, Ph.D., CFA, you have to assess your personal feelings about risk. If you are willing to take a risk on an opportunity to earn a greater return, then the reinvestment of equity may be for you. It is simple to find investments that earn more on an after-tax basis than the after-tax cost of a mortgage, according to Taylor. For example, if the after-tax cost is 4 percent, it is reasonable to expect more than a 4 percent return on many investment options on an after-tax basis, which illustrates the possibility that investing mortgage money will put you ahead of the game.

Conservatives

Conservative investors are more risk-averse than other types of investors. Conservatives tend to put their money into low-risk investments such as bonds, mutual funds, and savings accounts. The less risky an investment or account type is, the lower the rate of return that an investor has the opportunity to earn. For conservative investors, it is more about preserving the principal than it is to grow the account or earn an income off their money. Many conservative investors do not use the equity in their home or business to invest in other purposes because they feel that it puts their home in jeopardy. They feel it makes their home vulnerable if, for some reason, they were to invest their equity funds and the investment does not provide a big enough return to cover the payments required on the equity line, loan, or mortgage. This does not mean that some conservative investors do not use the equity in their properties to invest in other ways, but they are less likely to do so than riskier investors tend to.

Risk takers

Risk takers are the least averse to taking risk and will lay all of their money on the line if it means they have a chance to earn more money off it on another investment. This group of investors is the first to use any capital (including leveraging home equity funds) they have access to. They are willing to invest in higher risk accounts made up of stocks or to start a business venture. The riskier the investment, the higher rate of return, but high-risk investments tend to produce a greater return on the investment than lower-risk investments. A few high-risk investments are options to buy stocks and mutual funds made up of volatile, high-risk stocks.

Middle-of-the-roaders

Investors who are not conservative but are not quite risk-takers are considered to be middle-of-the-road investors. These investors are willing to take a moderate amount of risk, so they are more likely to use equity in a property to invest than conservatives. When they invest this money, it is typically in moderately safe investments, where there is an opportunity to preserve the majority of their capital but also an opportunity to grow their capital and earn income from it. To determine your risk level, here are a few questions to ask yourself:

- **What is your time horizon for the investment?** Can you invest the money for 20 years, or do you need the return on your investment next year? The longer you have to invest, the more risk you can take because you have a longer timeframe to recoup any losses.

- **How much capital can you lose without having financial issues?** The theory is that you should only invest the amount of money you can afford to lose. The less money you have, the less risk you can take. The more money you have, the more risk you can take.

Once you know what your risk level is, it can help you to better determine if using the equity in your home is something you would be comfortable doing. It also helps steer you to the type of investments you may be most comfortable investing in. Now it is time to do your homework and learn how to put that money to good use for you and your future.

Investment Options

There is a plethora of ways you can use your equity funds. Before you write a check from your equity, think about the purchase you are about to make. Then ask yourself the following questions and jot down your answers. It is important that you think through your investment before you run out and put your money down.

Questions to ask yourself about your investment:

- Is the purchase a necessity?
- Is the item a declining asset?
- Is it an asset that can earn money over time?
- Is this a risky investment or more of a conservative investment?
- Does the risk of the investment match your risk level?
- Does your investment in this asset propel you toward reaching your goal?

Declining assets that lose value when used or over a period of time and cannot bring you a good (if any) return include:

- Cars
- Trucks
- Boats
- Motorcycles
- Vacations
- Recreational vehicles (RVs)
- Clothes and other material items

Appreciating assets that increase in value over time and can bring you a return on your money include:

- Real estate property (land, residential, commercial, agricultural, industrial)
- Business (starting a new one or growing an existing one)
- Private mortgages (bring you interest payments and provide a monthly income)
- Home improvements and renovations (increase the value of your home)
- Retirement investments (fund a nest egg for your golden years)
- College educations (bring you or the person you are paying for more money in their careers)
- Paying off bad debt (gives you with more money and less debt in the long run)
- Insurance (protects what you own, and some forms bring you cash payments)

- Stock, bond, and mutual fund portfolios (depending on the investments, it can bring you monthly income or long-term access to cash)

Each of the appreciating assets is covered in the following chapters. Each chapter covers the investment option in great detail. You will learn about the benefits and possible drawbacks for each of these options. You will also learn how to invest your equity money into each of these investments, including resources you can turn to in order to help you invest your money wisely.

If your investments are not diversified and are only one-dimensional, then when and if that investment declines, you may lose all of your money. A good example of is the dot-com boom that took place in the 1990s. Silicon Valley was booming with technology businesses such as computer hardware and software companies. Personal computer use was taking off, and many investors were buying up the stocks of these technology companies. Some investors only purchased technology stocks, and many of the employees of the technology companies received stock options as a benefit of being employees of the company. The technology stocks continuously increased, and many personal and employees investors made millions of dollars over a several-year period. Because the technology stocks were doing so well, many of these investors only owned technology stocks or had the majority of their investment portfolio in technology stocks.

However, when entrepreneurs and would-be business owners saw how well these technology companies were doing, more and more technology businesses entered the market. By 2000, the technology market was saturated. The majority of these businesses were not standing on solid ground but rather were opened and running in an overnight operation that did not have a solid business or marketing plan in place. The main concern of these companies was to drive mass amounts of traffic to the business Web site and eventually take the company public (called an initial public offering, or IPO). When a company goes public, it can then sell stocks in the stock market, which attracts the general public and can help to make the company even more profitable.

With a saturated market in 2000, the success of these technology companies declined at a rapid rate because there were just too many of them in the market, and some companies were not being run effectively and efficiently. Technology stocks started to and continued to decline until many of these stocks became worthless. Not only did the majority of these technology businesses close, but all of the investors who had a majority or only technology stocks watched as their investment portfolio that was once worth millions of dollars dwindled to next to nothing.

Investing is a journey – whether it is a short or long journey is up to you. You create your own journey with the type of investments you choose. Some investment options are slow and steady, making them less risky. But the slow and steady investments do not tend to provide as great of a return on your investment than other riskier investments can bring. Examples of slow and steady investments are savings accounts, money market funds, and bonds. Then there are investment vehicles that are seen as wealth-building investments. These types of investments are riskier, but they can also produce a greater return on your money than the interest paid on the balance in a standard savings account. Examples of these include stocks, real estate, and starting or buying a business.

MARKETS
QUARTER DOLLAR
LIBERTY
IN GOD WE TRUST

Your investment horizon, or how many years you have to invest your money, plays as important a role in your investment choices as how much risk you are willing to take. If you are in your early 20s and plan on retiring when you are 59 ½, then you can take more risks than someone who is in their mid-40s who has less time than you to do until they retire. Someone in their early 20s has more time to recoup any losses from their investments and still meet their long-term investment goals – a recuperation that is much harder for someone who is closer to retirement. The length of your investment is not only about reaching your retirement goal, either. If you are investing money now to make enough money to send your child to college, then your investment horizon is only as long as you have until you need to turn the investment into cash by selling the investments in order to pay for your child's college education costs.

In the end, the types of investments you choose are based on three major factors. First, it is about your personal risk tolerance or how much risk you are willing to take. Second, investments are chosen by how many years (or how long) you have to invest. Finally, the types of investments you choose should be aligned with your overall investment goals – whether the investment performs well in the long run, or what the investment rate of return is if your investment goal has a short timeframe.

Diversification

This is also a good time to mention diversification of your investments. Diversification is one of the most important factors of being a savvy investor because each type of investment carries a different risk. Whether the risk is high or low depends on the investment itself, and risk is the main factor for diversifying your investments.

Diversification involves using your equity to invest in several different investments, rather than using all of your money to invest in only one vehicle. Diversification helps protect your initial investment and your return. If your investments are properly diversified, when and if one of your investments dips in value, your losses are offset by your other investments that remain steady or are increasing in value. For example, if your portfolio of investments includes a stock portfolio, some real estate property, and a new loan modification business you started with your equity funds, you have your money diversified in several different investments. While real estate and stocks may be down in the current market, your loan modification business is bringing in a tremendous profit in a declining market. Your business income is offsetting the losses you may be taking on your real estate and stocks. If you own a business that is not volatile, where seasons or markets do not affect its performance, then there may be times when your business, real estate, and stock portfolio investments are all doing well and making you money. In general, when the economy as a whole is performing well, then these are the times when most investments perform well, too.

If you do not diversify but have all of your investments in one place, and that investment fails, then all of your money will be gone. For example, if you used all of your money to buy real estate, then when the real estate and housing market tanked in 2007 and 2008, you may have lost all of your potential return on your investment.

Get Ready, Get Set, Go

You have learned what equity is and how you can access it. You also have a basic overview of the types of investments you can put your equity funds into. You understand there are appreciating and depreciating assets. Now you have a foundation of knowledge on which you can build from. Your next step is to learn about each of the investment options available to you in detail before investing your money in any of them. Get ready, get set, and invest.

Checklist	
✓	Make a list of the ways you are interested in using your equity funds
✓	Determine if these options are appreciating or depreciating assets
✓	Project what the return on investment is that you expect from each option
✓	Decide if you want to invest all of your funds in one option or if you would like to spread your investment over several different options
✓	Determine how risky your investment option is and if it is possible to lose all of your money in the investment
✓	If it is possible to lose all of your money in the investment, then it is important to evaluate how this will affect your financial situation
✓	Assess whether the investment options you are considering and the projected returns on these investments help you work toward your goal

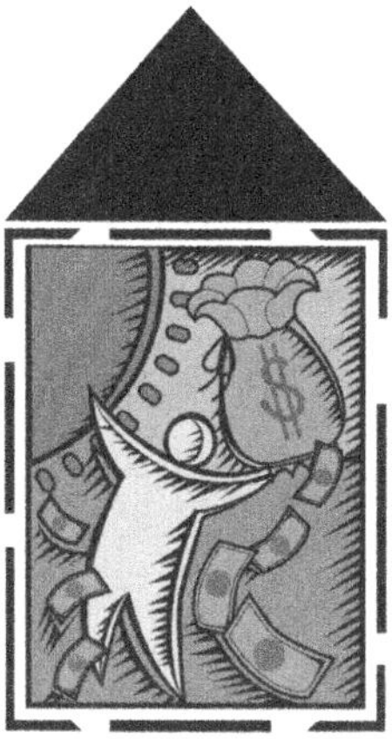

CHAPTER 6

Start a Business

In this chapter you will:

- Discover three ways you can investment your money in business ventures
- Learn about the costs of starting and running a business
- Determine how to use your equity to invest in a business venture
- Calculate or measure the estimated return on your investment
- Learn what steps you need to take to protect your investment and ensure a return

Millions of new businesses are started each year in the United States. Some of these businesses are started because employees are laid off from their corporate jobs; others are started to fill a need that is not being filled by current businesses. This chapter discusses how you can leverage your equity funds to start and run a new business. Starting a new business is one of the top ways that people have built the greatest amount of wealth because businesses tend to be the investment vehicle that keeps on giving. However, it can also be very risky and will probably cost you the most amount of your equity in order to make it a successful investment. This chapter will also cover some of the costs of starting a business and how the equity funds can be used to invest in the new venture.

Invest in Your Own Career

If you have a product or service you can sell, using your equity money to pay for the start-up costs of your own business can be profitable and fulfilling. You may consider using your equity funds in starting a new business as an investment in your career. The start-up costs for a business can vary greatly depending on the type of business you plan to open. The idea of investing your equity funds into starting a new business is twofold. First, you are investing your money in a vehicle that has the potential to bring you a monthly income in the form of profits from the business operations. Second, opening and operating your own business creates and builds wealth over time. As millions of businesses are started each year, millions of businesses are sold each year, and millions of businesses fail each year as well. Not only can your business bring you monthly income, but it also may bring you a return on your investment if and when you sell it in the future.

If you are thinking about starting a new business, the first step you need to take is to determine which type of business you want to open. The possibilities are endless. You do not have to have a one-of-a-kind concept to start a business. It may be a type of business that already exists, such as a restaurant, dry cleaner, clothing store, or a tax service firm. Consider your skills and interests when deciding the type of business you are interested in opening. You may come up with a list of possibilities that you can investigate further before making a final decision. When making a final decision, take into consideration that those who invest money in a business based on their skills and interests tend to be more successful than those who invest in businesses they know nothing about or have no interest in learning about. You may also want to consider the market. Is there a need not being filled that your business idea can fill?

Market conditions can affect the success or failure of a business as well. You may be a wise businessperson and spend your equity money on only the necessities to make the business a success, but if market conditions hold your customers back from purchasing your products or services, your business may fail. For example, in hard economic times when unemployment is high, people tend to watch their spending very closely and only buy necessities. If your business is considered a luxury, or at least not a necessity, this can mean fewer customers and less income for you and your business. This means all of the money you have invested in the business is lost, and the future income and wealth the company could have brought you vanishes with the closing of the business. You also have the loan amount you pulled out in equity to consider because even though your business failed, you still owe the lender the money you used from your equity line of credit, equity loan, or cash-out refinance.

One business sector that may be severely affected by a bad housing market, for example, is the mortgage industry. If you are working in the mortgage industry when there is a major decline, which is what happened in the housing decline that started in 2007, then you may get laid off from your job. Instead of looking for a new mortgage broker position with another firm, you may be wise to apply your mortgage knowledge and experience to open a loan-modification business. Not only do you have the skills and experience to be able to open and run this business efficiently, but there is also a need for loan-modification businesses in a declining economy because economic problems cause an increase in the home foreclosure rate and increased difficulty in homeowners making their mortgage payments. A loan modification business fills a need that you can capitalize on.

CASE STUDY: DEALING WITH DEBT

William A. Kern, President
Dutchmaid Family of Laundromats

Like millions of Americans, William Kern and his wife found themselves swimming in the deep end of credit card debt. When they finally realized that their credit card debt was out of control, the collective amount of debt totaled $40,000 spread over three credit cards and a line of credit at their local credit union.

After considering their options, they turned to the home they had owned since 1973, refinancing it into a 30-year, fixed-rate mortgage. The refinance allowed them to use the equity they had built up in their home over the years to pay off all their credit card debt — turning the non-tax-deductible debt of consumer credit into a tax-deductible debt.

Using the 30-year mortgage to pay off the $40,000 in debt allowed the Kerns to decrease the total amount of interest they would pay in the long run. Because mortgage interest rates are much lower than credit card interest rates, it not only decreased the total amount they would pay in the long-term, but it also helped to chip away at the principal balance because more of a mortgage payment went toward principal than the minimum monthly credit card payment. Overall, it helped to create a more manageable cash flow situation.

In the process, Kern also decided he wanted to expand his laundromat business. Rather than run up their credit cards, they decided to use some of the equity he had built up in his IRA account. The laundromat investment was expected to bring William a return on his investment; then, with that return, he would expect to pay several times over the amount he originally pulled from his IRA.

Start-up Costs

Again, the start-up costs involved in starting a business can vary from business to business. Some businesses require very little in the way of initial costs to start the business, while other types of businesses require large sums of money. A freelance writing and editing business can be run from a home office and only require a computer, Internet access, Web site, telephone, and business cards. A restaurant, however, needs a building, a full kitchen, menus, glassware, silverware, plates, staff, and more to get going and operate successfully.

Some of the start-up and ongoing costs you need to consider when opening a business include:

Equipment: These costs can range from nothing to hundreds of thousands of dollars, depending on the type of business you are opening. For example, if you are starting a home-based Web store and you already own a computer, then you may not need to purchase any equipment. On the other hand, if you are opening an ice cream store, then you need to purchase ice cream freezer display cases, blenders, scoopers, and storage freezers. This would mean an initial equipment cost in the tens of thousands of dollars.

Building/office space: Lease fees can be in the upper thousands of dollars a month, but if you are running a home-based business, such as a virtual assistant business, then you can literally do business from your dining room table or a spare bedroom in your home. If you are opening a frozen-food distribution company where you need thousands of square feet of warehouse space and office space for the operations and administrative side of the business, then you are probably looking at thousands and possibly tens of thousands of dollars to obtain a warehouse and office space.

Staff/employees: If you are a one-man (or woman) show, then you may not have any costs associated with hiring. If you are opening a business such as a restaurant that requires cooks, wait staff, a cashier, and other employees, then you are going to need enough money to pay their hourly wages, employee taxation, and workers' compensation coverage each week, which can quickly add up to tens of thousands of dollars, depending on how big of a restaurant it is. Obviously, the more staff you have to employ to run the business, the more money you are going to need to cover these costs.

Office supplies: From printer ink cartridges and paper clips to copier paper and pens, most companies need some kind of a stash of office supplies for daily business operations. For a freelance writer who works from a home office, there may be very little need for office supplies — possibly only a couple of ink cartridges and one ream of paper a year (amounting to approximately $100 per year). On the other side of the spectrum, a financial services firm that invests money for clients and has a staff of 100 investors needs pens, company forms, paperclips, printer paper, ink cartridges, sticky notes, rubber bands, and file folders to name but a few items. The office supplies bill for running this type of office on a monthly basis is probably going to be thousands of dollars.

Marketing materials (business cards, letterhead, envelopes): A Web-based business such as an Internet marketing consultant or search engine optimization (SEO) service provider may not need to purchase any print marketing supplies. The business cards would be electronic, contracts would be sent to clients via e-mail, company bills paid online, and newsletter and promotional pieces would also be sent e-mail. A mail-order business, on the other hand, needs packing slips, shipping boxes printed with the company name, invoices, postcards for direct mailings, paper catalogs for clients to order from, and the list continues from there. While the SEO expert may have a very small marketing expense, the mail-order business probably spends tens of thousands of dollars each month for all of these items.

Web site: If you are a do-it-yourselfer, you can get a business Web site up and running with just a little bit of your time. You can buy a domain name for as little as $1.99 per year and up to about $35 per year, depending on the company you choose. One of the biggest domain companies in existence is **www.GoDaddy.com**. Other business owners turn to professional Web site designers and pay a couple thousand to $100,000 on a Web site design (depending on the inner pages and complexity of the site). For example, if you are opening an e-commerce store similar to Amazon.com then you may have hundreds of pages of products, and you also need a shopping cart added to your site so customers can place orders and your business can process them.

Computer(s): Computers can run about $400 to $3,000 each, depending on the amount of memory and functions you need on the computer, as well as the number of computers you need (one for each employee).

Furniture and fixtures: Office spaces or stores that need to be completed with furnishings can quickly add up to tens of thousands of dollars. For example, if you are opening an interior design business and you are opening a retail space in an office complex where you can meet with clients and store purchases you make for clients, then you are going to need to furnish your space. Some office rentals come as blank slates, where the walls and floors are unfinished with only an open room. This is typically the case when the lease unit is new. This means that you have to pay to put in the carpet, put up the drywall, paint the walls, and put the toilet and the sink in the bathroom. This is on top of the office furniture you need – a desk, a chair, chairs for clients to sit in, pictures and paintings for the wall, and other office décor. Previously rented units may have carpet and bathroom fixtures already installed, so all you would need to pay for is office furniture.

Licenses and certifications: Depending on your profession, licensing for the business starts at $150 and goes up from there.

Advertising and marketing: You may have the best business, product, or service ever created, but if nobody knows it exists, then you may have a hard time attracting customers. The types of marketing and advertising options vary as much as the costs. For example, if you are opening a plumbing business, you may be able to start your marketing with a $600 ad in the yellow pages of your local area phonebook. This and referrals from previous clients may be all you need to generate enough business for your company. If you are opening a tax preparation business, you may want to purchase billboards, TV commercials, radio ads, and online banners that are focused on the local area that you cover. This can shoot your advertising bill up to $20,000, rather than the $600 that the plumber has to spend.

Utility expenses: Home offices may change your home utility bill by less than $100 because you are at home working rather than working out of the home now. If you run a clothing store, then your electric bill may run you $300 per month for lighting and air conditioning or heating the store. An ice cream business or restaurant that also has refrigerators, stoves, ovens, and freezers on top of lighting, air conditioning, and heating may have a $1,000 utility bill.

Phone and Internet bills: If you are adding a business line to your home and already have Internet, then your cost to start your business in this area may only run you a few hundred dollars. On the other hand, if you are opening a call center where each employee has to have Internet access and you need a complex phone system, it could cost you $10,000 to get your operation up and running with phones and Internet.

Costs can vary significantly based on the type of business you are opening. Generally speaking, there are businesses, such as a freelance writing business, a lawn care service, or an online retail store that you can start for less than $500. Then there are businesses, such as restaurants, hair salons, and a florist shop that can cost over $100,000 to start.

CASE STUDY: COVERING THE COSTS

Randy Mitchelson, Owner
National Web Leads LLC
www.mortgagebyrandy.com
www.nationalwebleads.com

CLASSIFIED CASE STUDIES™
directly from the experts

After a successful career as a regional manager for Bank of America and other leadership positions in large financial institutions, such as CIBC and KeyBank, Randy Mitchelson decided he wanted to own a business of his own. In fact, Mitchelson went on to open two businesses of his own, Mortgage by Randy and National Web Leads. His business, National Web Leads, uses the latest in online media advertising techniques to generate consumer finance referrals for businesses in the financial services industries. Mortgage by Randy allows Randy to continue to use his mortgage experience and financial knowledge to help his own clients rather than the clients of a bank or financial institution, where he is simply an employee.

As someone who knows the ins and outs of making financially beneficial decisions, Mitchelson decided his best option for starting his businesses was to use his home equity to help fund the endeavors. Mitchelson saw a lot of other people using the equity in their homes to buy "toys" such as boats and big TVs. This is not what he was looking for; his goal was to create a cushion for emergencies and to use it as needed for business purposes.

Not only did the equity Mitchelson pulled from his home create cash flow during the start-up of his new business, but he was also able to invest in short-term, private mortgages for people rehabbing properties; invest in real estate projects in the Dominican Republic; and use some of the funds to make home improvements on his primary residence. Mitchelson has benefited from the wise use of his home equity to invest for his tomorrow. So far, he has earned revenue through the private mortgages he invested in and has been able to sustain his new businesses by having access to the equity line so as not to impact the cash flow of the business. The Dominican Republic investments are part of Randy's long-term strategy so it is too early to cite the results of this investment, but the projects do seem promising.

Buy a Franchise

Another option for starting your own business is to buy a franchise. The benefit of buying a franchise is you are buying into a "turnkey" business model, which helps to ensure success. For example, if you buy a SUBWAY® restaurant, you are buying an already established business model. Not only does this franchise have a manual of information you can follow and use as a guide to run your business, but you are also opening a recognizable business. The fact that it is a well-known brand can help you to attract customers that a mom-and-pop store or sandwich shop may not be able to do. And this is true of almost any franchise that you purchase. Franchise investors receive training, materials, and guidelines to follow. Because the business methodology has already been established, you have less of a chance of your business failing than if you try to start a business from scratch. Franchises help investors avoid making mistakes that can cost them time and money — and put your investment at risk for loss.

Purchasing a franchise requires an upfront investment in cash and offers various financing options for covering the remaining balance. Some franchisors offer financing through the franchise itself. While most do require you to put some kind of down payment on the purchase of a franchise, you can use one of their financing options to make monthly payments to cover the rest of the amount you owe for the purchase. Because most of these financing options have interest rates that are higher than an equity line, loan, or mortgage, your other option is to use the equity from your property to pay for the down payment, or in some cases, you may even have enough equity to buy the franchise outright without the need to finance the purchase with the franchisor.

One thing to be aware of: Your franchise investment does not end with the purchase. Part of being a franchise owner also requires you to pay an annual fee, and some franchises require you to pay a percentage of your profits as well. Even with the costs associated with buying, running, and operating a franchise, it can be a lucrative way of running a successful business without figuring out how to start your own business and build your own brand.

If you are considering investing in a franchise, check out the "Is Franchising for Me?" workbook from the Small Business Administration (SBA) at **www.sba.gov**, and click on the Business Planner tab.

Buy an Existing Business

Another option for investing your equity funds is to buy an existing business, which is a business that is up and running but is not a franchise. These can be individually owned businesses where the owners are selling the business to you directly, or can even be medium- or large-sized businesses or corporations. Buying a business that is already functioning reduces some of the risk because the current business owner can show you the current revenues and expenses of the business. If your skills are running and managing a business, rather than starting from scratch, then buying an existing business may be the right move for you.

There are costs, of course, involved in buying an existing business, but it alleviates you from paying initial start-up costs, and it relieves you from the challenge of launching a new business. Some of the initial expenses include the cost of your time, and you can also use your equity monies to cover your personal paycheck for running and operating the business. Some business owners hold off on actually paying themselves until the business turns a profit, so you may not want to use your equity funds as your personal income. Finding the right business for you may take months or years of your time. Before you make a final decision on the purchase, you will have expenses involved in evaluating the business as well. These types of fees can include costs for a financial advisor to professionally inspect the financials of the business and the legal fees for having an attorney draw up the legal agreement for the purchase of the business.

This is not to mention the cost of purchasing the business from the current owner. Good businesses do not come cheap. The better off a business is, the more money a seller can demand for it. There are also problems that can come along with buying an existing business that do not have anything to do with the money. The policies, procedures, and existing employees typically transfer from the previous owner to you, the new owner. This may seem like it makes operating the business easier, but the problems that existed with the previous owner simply transfer to the new owner. This means you have to have the ability to make decisions, even if they are hard decisions, such as firing people and influencing the employees to do things your way.

The way you manage and run your new business directly relates to the return you are going to receive on your investment. You can either run the business to success, where you are bringing in more money than you are paying out in expenses (including your repayment of the equity line or equity financing funds you used to buy and operate the business to start with), or you can run the business into the ground. When you are running a franchise, there is less of a chance for failure because the franchisor provides you with proven methods (a quintessential blueprint) for running the business. This does not mean that franchises do not fail, because they do if franchisees do not follow the guidelines; if the location of the franchise does not attract the right customers; or for a myriad of other reasons.

When you buy an existing business that has achieved success in the past, there may also be somewhat of a guideline you can follow. The past owner has run the company in a way that has brought it to a successful place up to the point that you bought it. If you continue to run the business the same way then you may have a better chance of succeeding also. On the other hand, if you buy a business that is just getting by or is failing, you may be able to infuse your own management style of operational guidelines to improve it. Buying an existing business gives you a baseline to work from that is different from starting a business from scratch or even opening a new location of a franchise operation.

Invest in Someone Else's Business

If you like the idea of investing your money in a business that you do not have to start yourself or operate on your own, then investing in someone else's business may be the right vehicle for you. On a 2009 episode of ABC's "Ugly Betty," this exact concept was portrayed. A once-fledgling magazine publishing company ran into hard times because of the economy and needed funds to get back on track. A business investor gave them the funds required to continue operations, and an agreement was worked out where the investor receives a percentage of the business profits on top of the repayment of his initial investment. This may be a TV show, but this scenario happens every day.

It may seem like a win-win situation, but there are some drawbacks to investing in a business that is owned and operated by someone else. First, it can be difficult to find and analyze a business that is a good investment. You have to continue to think about the end goal, which is for you to invest money in a business that you are going to profit from. This requires a great deal of research and analysis such as assessing the financial statements of the company as well as the business strategies of the company. If you are an accountant or a finance whiz, then this is an analysis that you may be able to do on your own. Most individuals, however, hire an accountant to review and make an assessment of the financial statements of the company to analyze how well (or how bad) it is doing.

Second, the challenge comes with finding a business worth investing in to begin with. Companies looking for private funding do not put an ad on the Internet in hopes of finding the right investor. The best privately held companies that are looking for investors turn to networking as the primary source. This means if you are not running in the right circles, you may miss out on these prime investment opportunities. If you are interested in investing your money in private firms, the best place to seek out these opportunities is by talking with financial advisers, tax experts, and legal professionals. These experts are great matchmakers between investors and those seeking investors. If you have a business attorney, accountant, or financial advisor you work with, then contact them and talk with them about the type of business you are looking to buy.

If you do not know legal professionals, financial advisors, or accountants, you can turn to the Yellow Pages of your local phone book or one in the city where you are looking to buy a business. Call some of the professionals in your local area and tell them what kind of business you are looking to buy and see if this is a service they provide, or if they know of someone you may be able to talk to. If they cannot help you, they may be able to refer you to someone else who can help you.

These groups of professionals also have association meetings and social gatherings you can attend to mix and mingle. Your local newspaper prints local calendar events where you can search for events where these types of professionals might be in large groups. You can also contact the legal bar association for the state where you are looking to buy a business. For example, the Florida Bar has a list of local events in different cities scattered throughout the state.

How to Use Your Equity to Pay for Costs

Once you access the equity in your property, you will be able to use these funds to pay for the start-up and operational costs of running or investing in your business. How you access these funds depends on the type of financing you used to tap into your equity. For example, if you established a home equity line of credit, then the lender may have provided checks for you to access these funds. You can either write a check to pay for each expense, or you can deposit an equity check into a business bank account that you can then use to pay for business expenses. Then, you will be able to access the funds on an ongoing basis from your business account.

If you used a cash-out refinance to access the equity, then you received a check at closing for the amount of equity you accessed. You can deposit this check into your personal account, then write a check from your personal account to fund the business account. Then you will be able to access the funds on an ongoing basis from your business account. Because the personal equity line is going to be made payable to you, you are not going to be able to deposit a check with your name on it into a business account. When you deposit it into your personal account, you can write a check from the personal account in order to fund the opening of the business account. Even if you are the president of the company, banks do not typically let you deposit checks made out in your personal name into a business account. The only exception is if your name and the business name are the same.

How Your Investment Pays Off

The entire premise of a business is to turn a profit and make money. So before you invest your equity funds into starting a business, it is important that the returns you are projecting from the business investment are worth the risk you are taking for investing the funds in the first place. Then, it is about creating a successful business that reaches or exceeds your projected returns.

There are several steps that go into creating and building a successful business. However, the bottom line is, if you invest your home equity funds into starting a business, buying an existing business, or investing in someone else's business, how does this provide you with a return on your investment?

First, you have to consider the fact that you have to cover the monthly payment that is due on the financing method you used to initially access the equity; so, at the very least, your business should be turning enough of a profit to make this payment each and every month. The good news is that this is a pre-tax cost and does not take into consideration the tax benefits of the mortgage or equity line. It also does not take into consideration the tax benefits of being a business owner.

Then you have to consider the costs of running the business. These may include covering expenses such as marketing, utilities, phone, or rent. If you run your business from home, then these costs may be minimal. After you cover all of the costs of doing business, what is left over is profit. Profit is your return on your investment. Again, this is prior to taking all of the tax breaks and write-offs you accumulate as a business owner, which allows you to pay out less and keep more of your money. You also earn a return on your investment if and when you sell the business for more than your initial investment and what you owe on the business. In order to fully understand the tax breaks and write-offs that you may be able to take into consideration, it is wise for you to consult a tax or financial advisor. You can also access the IRS Web site at **www.irs.gov** to learn how these deductions work and whether or not the deductions apply to your personal financial situation.

Is investing in a business a risky investment? The short answer is yes; any investment that requires you to put your money into it has risk associated with it. Investing in a business creates an investment situation where you can lose everything you have put into the business, but it can also create a situation where you can create the greatest amount of wealth. When starting or running a business, it is about more than the money you invest in it. It is also about your management and business skills, making wise business decisions that create the ideal return on investment for your money. It is one of the only investment options where you have control of what happens.

Is investing your equity funds in a business a great investment or an opportunity to lose it all? It depends on you, but it does have the ability to bring you wealth for years to come. Businesses fail every day due to various influences. Whether it is because you made a bad decision about how you spent your marketing budget or you hired the wrong employees to help you build your business, these all factor in to how much of a return your investment brings. There are also outside forces that can have an effect on how well your business does. So, before launching your next great business idea, buy a franchise, or purchase an existing business, you want to assess your abilities to start and run a successful business. Working on your own is completely different from working for someone else. When you are an employee, a paycheck comes regularly when you show up and do your job. When you are self-employed, it is more than showing up and doing what someone else tells you to do. Being self-employed is about being motivated and having the ability to tell yourself and others what to do to make it a successful operation.

Does your return on investment change if you are investing in someone else's business? It can. There are different factors involved in investing your money into a business being run by someone else because you lose some of the control you have in making the business succeed. It also depends on your investment agreement. For example, if you are a silent investor, you do not have a say in how the business is run, even though how the business is run has a direct effect on the profits or loss of the business.

Your agreement may allow you to offer an opinion or dictate how your funds are invested, but because you are not the business owner, you do not have control over the business decisions made and all of the other factors that make or break a business. Alternatively, if your management skills are not at their best, and you are investing a business run by a savvy business owner, it may create the ultimate win-win situation. It does not matter that your business skills are lacking because you are investing in the business owner's ability to successfully run his business, turn a profit, and hand over your percentage of the profit. The amount of the profit you receive is negotiated between you and with the investor, and it depends on the amount of money you invest. The smaller the amount of money you invest in the company, the smaller your percentage of the profits will most likely be and vice versa. Investing in a business, whether starting your own or investing in someone else's, has a risk associated with it. This is not any different from the risk associated with investing your money in other investment vehicles.

Checklist	
✓	Determine if you have a business idea or service or product to offer
✓	Consider the motivation, skills, and knowledge that running a business requires
✓	Determine the monetary investment amount you have to make to start your business
✓	If you are interested in buying an existing business or investing in someone else's business, contact and network with financial advisors, tax advisors, and legal professionals to help you find ideal businesses for sale and business investment opportunities
✓	Project a realistic return on your investment from the business
✓	Consider the expected return and determine if it is enough to offset the risk of losing a portion or all of your initial investment

SAVINGS BOND
OF AMERICA
DOLLARS

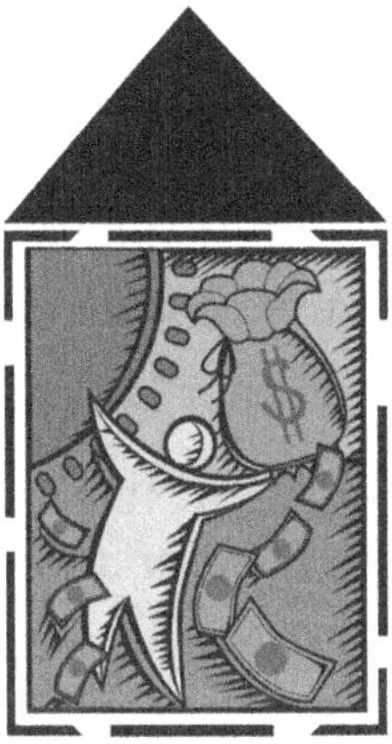

CHAPTER 7

Invest in Real Estate

In this chapter you will:

- Learn how to use equity in a property you own to buy more real estate
- Discover ways to increase cash flow, equity, or both
- How to find properties that will increase your cash flow, increase your equity standing, or both
- Uncover the advantages and disadvantages of investing in each type of property

A declining or depressed housing market and real estate environment can be the perfect time to invest in real estate. Sales prices are at bargain-basement discounts, meaning you pay less upfront — invest less of your equity funds now — and as the value of the property increases, it causes the return on your investment — when you sell your property — to be greater in the long run. This chapter covers the various options available to you for buying residential and commercial properties now while the cost is lower and what this can mean for your return on investment in the long run. It will cover buying single-family homes or duplexes and four-unit properties that you could use as rental properties. It will also cover other types of properties such as mixed-use residential, office buildings, apartment buildings, and other types of commercial properties you could buy for investment purposes. The beauty of it is that you are financing the purchase of a new piece of real estate with the equity of an existing piece of property – you do not have to dip into your savings. Instead, you are leveraging the cash you already have built up in an existing property to expand your real estate portfolio.

It is All About the Cash Flow

When you buy real estate for investment purposes, you have two goals. Your first goal is create cash flow, which is the profit left after you cover all of the expenses of owning the property. Your second goal is to profit from the sale of the property by selling it for more than you paid for it when you bought it. Income on the property is the money you are receiving from renting the property out. The costs associated with owning and maintaining a property can be deductions from the profit, which may include the monthly equity line payment, landscaping fees, and maintenance costs. Investing your equity funds in real estate can be lucrative because it creates cash flow; it appreciates in value, allowing you to earn a profit on your investment either when you sell the property or if you pull equity out of the property, and the IRS provides tax benefits to real estate investors, which is where the Cash Equivalent Benefits fit into the equation.

There are special benefits that real estate investors receive that the standard property owner does not benefit from. These benefits permit real estate investors to deduct the expenses for operating the property from the rent collected (or the income produced from the property). Real estate investors can also deduct the capital they invest in any assets that depreciate (such as machinery and equipment used for the business), the interest that is paid for financing the property, or any money that is borrowed against the property.

This may be Greek to you, but watch how this benefits you as a real estate investor:

You decide to buy an office building that has ten office suites that you rent out to local businesses. The purchase price of the building is $1,000,000. To you, the total cost of the property is $1,000,000. To the IRS, your purchase is broken up into appreciating and depreciating categories; it separates the purchase price into the cost for the land ($200,000); the cost for the furniture, fixtures, and equipment (FF&E, $300,000); and the building itself ($500,000). While the land value is not depreciable, the FF&E and building are depreciating assets — depreciating assets that you can use as a tax write-off. The end result is that depreciation reduces your taxable income from the property. The amount that the depreciation reduces your taxable income varies from situation to situation; so there is not a blanket calculation that everyone can use, but you can depreciate the FF&E and the building, and each year you can take the cost of depreciation and deduct it from your taxable income. It is like getting free money.

For example, you purchase a commercial building that costs you $2 million, and the cost is broken down for tax purposes as $300,000 for the land, $700,000 for FF&E, and $1 million for the building itself. While the land portion of the purchase is not depreciable, the FF&E and the building do have a depreciation value. The FF&E depreciates over a five-year period, while the structure depreciates over a period of 27.5 years. To calculate the appreciation value for each year, divide the total value by the number of years allowable for depreciation.

Asset value / Years to depreciate = Yearly appreciation value
FF&E: $700,000 / 5 = $140,000
Building: $1,000,000 / 27.5 = $36,363.64

When you subtract the building depreciation from the FF&E depreciation, you can find that the total amount of depreciation you could deduct for the first five years you own the property.

FF&E yearly appreciation - Building yearly appreciation = 5-year total depreciation
$140,000 – $36,363.64 = $103,636.36

Let us assume that your taxable income is $280,000 per year. According to the IRS, you can deduct the allowable amount for depreciation from your annual taxable income in order to decrease your overall taxable income, which in turn will decrease the amount of taxes that you will pay.

Annual taxable income - 5-year depreciation = Taxable income after depreciation
$280,000 – $103,636.36 = $176,363.64

To find out more about the tax deductibility of depreciation, visit the IRS Web site for small businesses at **www.irs.gov/businesses/small**.

Using Equity Allows You to Leverage Your Money

By using the equity funds from your existing piece of real estate to purchase an investment property, you are not only creating a source of cash flow, but you are also maximizing your cash flow. In essence, you are boosting the amount of money you can earn from the property by using someone else's money to make it happen – you are using the equity you have built in another property to buy the property outright, or to use as a source of cash for paying the down payment and closing costs. Instead of sitting on the pile of money that home equity represents, you are pulling this money out of the home. The home equity line or mortgage lender is giving you their money to use to buy another property.

However, your goal is not to buy the new property outright, because then all of your money will be sitting in a piece of real estate again, and this entire book is about how sitting on a pile of money may not be the wisest investment option. If you use the equity from one property to purchase a new property outright, then you have basically moved your equity from one property to another. You want your equity to do more than just sit in another piece of property.

The goal for investing in a new piece of property, therefore, is to use the home equity funds to put a cash down payment on the purchase of the new property and then finance the rest of the purchase price. This creates a double-dip opportunity for you. The interest portion of the home equity payment is usually fully tax-deductible; the depreciation of the building and the interest for the mortgage used to finance the purchase is also a tax deduction. So when you use the equity from your first property to purchase the second property, you are leveraging the lenders' money twice — one time to pull the equity out of the existing property, and again to finance the purchase of the second property. You are using someone else's money to purchase an asset that also provides you with income. Because you will lease out the investment property, as long as the lease fee is more than your cost to pay for owning the property, then you are profiting from owning the property. It is a win-win situation.

It is also important to understand that you may not be able to purchase a new property outright because you may not have enough equity in your current property to buy the property. You cannot turn $30,000 in equity to purchase a $150,000 property. You do, however, have enough equity for a down payment and to cover the closing costs on the purchase of the new property. Because you are going to rent new property out, depending on how much you rent the property for, you may receive enough rent to cover your financing costs and have enough money left over to profit or create cash-flow from the property.

CASE STUDY: REAL EQUITY FOR REAL ESTATE PURCHASES

Jill Nussinow
Cookbook Author
www.theveggiequeen.com

Author of *The Veggie Queen* cookbook, Jill Nussinow, and her husband watched as the market value of their home in California continued to increase, which meant they had built up a great deal of equity in the home. Unfortunately, as the value of the property once went up, it eventually came back down. Though the amount of equity had decreased, Nussinow was still in a position where she had a great deal of equity built up in the property that she could use.

"Doing nothing with the money didn't make sense to us, especially since we can pay for it," she said.

Thinking about their future, they decided to buy a piece of raw land — undeveloped land that does not have a structure built on it. Because the value of property had declined, they were able to use the equity in their current residence to buy the land at a 50 percent discount from the market value. They hope to hold the property until they get closer to retirement and sell it for a profit, so they can eventually build their retirement home.

The final outcome is yet to be seen, but recently a property in the area sold for $30,000 more than the Nussinows paid for their land, and their property has a vested septic system, which makes the value even higher.

Sources of Cash Flow

You reap the return on your investment with investment properties while you own them and again when you sell them. If your investment property purchase and ownership is structured correctly, you start to earn a return on your investment right away. There are seven sources of cash flow from investment properties: rent payments from tenants, new rents, increased rents, reducing expenses, increased cost of living to increase rent, restructuring debt, and eliminating unnecessary expenses. How you handle each of these items directly affects your cash flow.

Rent payment(s)

Whether you are renting out a single-family home, where you are receiving one monthly rent payment, or renting out ten office suites in an office building, those monthly rent payments create cash flow. If you buy the property when tenants already occupy it, there are existing leases that have existing terms and conditions that you have to honor. Some of the terms and conditions in these leases can also increase your cash flow potential. For example, cost of living clauses automatically increase the rent due on an annual basis. This is a built-in cash flow increase because as time goes by, your income goes up.

New rental income

There are also ways you can actively create new rents to increase your cash flow. The three main ways you can accomplish this is creating a new use for the property, changing the types of tenants that rent the property, or adding square footage to the property.

When you buy a property for investment purposes, the purpose of the building depends on how the building is used. The use of the building can also dictate what amount of income you can derive from owning it. For example, commercially zoned buildings such as warehouses, office buildings, and retail shopping centers that are available for businesses to use can be purchased and occupied by the owner, or they can be rented out to increase the potential income from owning these types of properties. Typically, a real estate investor purchases these types of properties to rent or lease these properties out to tenants in an effort to generate income. On the residential side of real estate investment, an investor could derive additional income from purchasing and renting out single-family homes as well. So buying and renting out new properties is about creating new rental income.

One way that you can create new rents is to buy a building or piece of real estate, knock it down, and build a new property that has a new purpose — one that generates more rental income than the current building. For example, if you buy a warehouse space that only allows you to rent it to one tenant but knock the warehouse down and build a retail shopping center, now you can rent the different spaces out to different tenants and generate more income. Another way to accomplish the same goal is to remodel or renovate it in a manner that produces new rents. For example, if you purchase a motel, you can upgrade the units and turn it into an office complex, so you are creating new rents by increasing the transaction amount and term of the rents. Now instead of renting out the rooms to guests one or two nights at a time, you have created a consistent monthly income by renting out the units to business tenants with leases that generate monthly income for you typically on a long-term basis — the typical length of a business lease is five to ten years.

With either of these choices, there are some drawbacks. First, you have to be careful that when you rebuild or remodel, you do not allow the costs or expenses exceed the potential new rents you are creating. Second, you need to consider the costs of operating the new type of property. If remodeling or building costs and the costs for operating the new type of property are higher than the rents you can bring in, then it defeats your whole purpose. You are limited by the amount of money in equity you have to work with, so it is important to monitor what you are spending. What you spend should not outweigh the potential return you can receive in rents and increased value of the property.

Instead of doing an overhaul on the physical property, you can also create new rents by doing an overhaul of the tenants. Different neighborhoods have different demographics. Some neighborhoods are depressed areas, while others are steady-going. Then there are up-and-coming neighborhoods. While some neighborhoods once attracted low-income families, they may be going through a regeneration period where they are now attracting retired baby boomers who have disposable income to spend. If you own a retail shopping center with stores that once catered to low-income families, but the regeneration of the neighborhood is now attracting baby boomers, the businesses that once catered to low-income families will probably move out of the neighborhood, leaving your space empty. You now have an opportunity to rent out these spaces to businesses that now cater to the retired baby boomer generation. Now you can attract businesses that you can charge a higher rent.

You may not be able to control what happens in the neighborhood once you buy a building in it, but you can control where you invest your money and how you use the property in response to what is going on the neighborhood. So, in the case mentioned above, you are investing money in a building in an area that is now attracting baby boomers. This type of investment choice can mean an increase in rental amounts and income for you.

A third way you can create new rents is to add rental square footage to the building. More square footage allows you to rent an individual unit out for more money. Adding additional square footage that creates new units allows you to rent out to additional tenants, which generates more income in rent. For example, if you own a set of warehouses, you could add square footage to each unit by building a small office in the front of each warehouse unit. This allows you to rent out the office space and warehouse space to business that have a need for this mixed-use property type. For example, an auto parts business may need to store its parts in the warehouse but also needs space for the owner to run the administrative side of the business in the office space. Another example is an event décor designer who needs the office space to meet with prospective clients but also needs a warehouse to store the décor and creations that have been built and used at weddings, parties, and other major social events.

Increase rental amount(s)

You always have the option to increase your return on your investment by increasing the amount you charge your tenants for rent. This may occur because you buy a property where tenants have been charged rents below market value by the previous owner. When you take ownership of the property, you can increase the rents to meet current market rates. It is possible to increase rents in the middle of a lease, but your ability to do this depends on which state the property is located and what the lease states. Rent amounts can also be increased when the lease is up for renewal, which is probably the more common way for landlords in most states to increase rent.

You can also increase rental amounts on an annual basis as the cost of living increases. It is also appropriate to increase rent as you upgrade the property. A new office suite may command a higher monthly lease amount than an office suite that is 20 years old.

It is important to note here that you have to be in tune with what is going on the market and neighborhood where your property is located. If the area is going through a downturn, you may have to keep the rental amounts status quo. Alternatively, if the neighborhood is going through a regeneration process, and tenants are standing in line to rent properties in the area, then you can increase rental amounts. It is a simple case of supply and demand.

Reduce expenses

Another way to increase the amount of money you earn on your property is to decrease the expenses of the property. It may be that the previous owner of the property outsourced management of the property to a property management company, but you plan on being a hands-on owner and manager. This is an automatic reduction on the operating expenses of the property, which is also an increase to your cash flow.

Maintenance costs and insurance costs are two more expenses that can eat into your cash flow, which ultimately deteriorates the return on your investment. Depending on the type of property, you may not need a full-time maintenance staff. It may be more cost-effective to outsource your maintenance on an as-needed basis. While you cannot outsource your insurance costs, you can shop around to find the best deal. You can use Web sites such as **www.BillSavings.com** to shop for and compare insurance policy pricing and features. If you already have a relationship with an insurance agent, you will also want to talk with them about any discounts you may be able to take advantage of by having more than one policy with them. Another source for information on various types of insurance is the Insurance Information Institute Web site at **www.iii.org**.

Insurance is a must when operating an investment property. It will cost you more in the long run if you end up getting sued, but there is no need to pay a higher premium than you have to for the coverage you need. So as you would for any major purchase, do some comparison-shopping for your insurance policy, too.

Increased cost of living

An increase in the cost of living allows you to raise rents, but it also increases your maintenance fees on an investment property. As the costs for products and services rise, it costs you more to run and maintain these types of properties. You can offset these costs by increasing rent amounts. If the building or property you own charges tenants maintenance fees, you can also charge a maintenance fee for use of the common areas of the property. This is more common with buildings that have business tenants, but you are probably familiar with maintenance fee concept if you have ever owned a condominium or townhouse in a community that is run by a condo or homeowners' association. If you own a shopping center, office building or complex, or other types of large rental properties, you can charge a maintenance fee on top of their monthly lease or rental amounts.

Eliminating expenses

There are also expenses of running the property that you may be able to get rid of completely. While you may not get away with not carrying insurance (because it is against the law when you have a mortgage on a property), you can do away with the added expense of holding monthly tenant events or providing cookies and coffee in the rental office. While these are added niceties, these items are not necessities for you to earn income on the property.

In order to determine which costs you may be able to eliminate, you will need to sit down with a complete list of the building or property expenses. Using your common sense, you can almost immediately pull out costs that are essential such as electricity, water, and insurance coverage, and whittle down the costs where you can without compromising the integrity of the rental property or business that you are running out of the property.

Restructuring debt

Another way to cut down expenses and increase your income on a property is to restructure the debt of the building or property. One of the primary ways to restructure debt is to refinance the mortgage on the property. Refinancing the mortgage can reduce the interest rate and monthly payment you are making. It may also help you to increase the term of the debt, which can help you reduce your monthly payments as well. In the long run, this may mean that you are paying more for the building over time, but refinancing is one way to reduce costs for the short-term.

There are other types of credit accounts that you may be able to restructure as well. You can either contact the individual creditor to negotiate a reduction in interest rate, payments, or terms, or you can consolidate your various debts into one debt. Establishing an equity line or doing a cash-out refinance to pull out enough equity from the building to pay off or reduce your outstanding debts can achieve this consolidation. Though this will not eliminate the debt completely, it can reduce the interest rate and payment you are charged, which can reduce your overall expenses on a monthly basis.

CASE STUDY: FROM AUTO GIANT TO CASH FLOW MERCENARY

Dennis P. Fassett
The Cash Flow Mercenary
www.cashflowmercenary.com

CLASSIFIED CASE STUDIES
directly from the experts

In 2003, Dennis Fassett was flying high with his corporate job in metro Detroit. Having been the director of an automotive supply company and expecting to reach vice president within the next two to three years, Fassett and his wife bought a big house, registered their four children in private school, and looked forward to their lucrative and stable lifestyle.

In late 2003, the first glimpse of problems, such as major budget cutbacks and layoffs in the automotive industry, started to appear in GM, Chrysler, and Ford. Rather than face the chance that these giants may fall, Fassett turned the other cheek. To compound the problem that was brewing, he bought GM stock in early January 2004. With GM stock at $55 per share — an all-time high — GM was poised to do great, and Fassett thought it was a wise investment to profit from.

The company Dennis worked for derived a large amount of its business from GM, so it started to retrench and retract late in the first quarter of 2004. With the rapid decline in the auto business by this time, Fassett's company tried to contract faster to keep its head above water, but it was too late. His department was cut, his staff was laid off, and he was reassigned to another department in the company. With auto stocks continuing to tumble, Fassett lost everything he had invested in the GM stock that previously looked so promising.

Fassett had four children, a stay-at-home wife, and an ill mother living with them to support, so he had to figure out a way to build a cushion for him and his family — fast. He finally settled on investing in real estate. After doing a great deal of research and educating himself on the real estate investment industry, he became convinced that in order to make money with real estate, he had to have money to start — whether it was his money or funds received from financing.

Though Fassett and his wife had cash reserves, they did not want to use their cash to invest in real estate. Instead, they opened a home equity line of credit on their current home to buy homes, do the repairs and fixes required to rehab the houses, then sell each home at a profit. After doing a couple of flips, Fassett used the proceeds from the sales as a down payment on the next purchase and to cover the cost of the repairs.

Then he started to use the equity line to put down payments on houses they bought to hold as rental properties. Once the homes were rented out, he did conventional cash-out refinances on each of the properties. He was buying the properties at reduced market values because of the depressed housing market, and doing the minor repairs allowed him to pull out all of their invested funds when the house appraised at a higher value.

For Fassett, the equity line was the critical factor in getting started in investing in and profiting from real estate.

Finding Properties That Offer Cash Flow and Equity Build-up Benefits

Your ultimate goal when buying a real estate investment is to find a property that not only brings you cash flow, but also builds up equity. You know the various ways equity builds in a property, but there are particular characteristics you can look for in a property that allows you to maximize your cash flow and equity buildup. The great news is that you do not have to recreate the wheel; hundreds of thousands of real estate investors have already paved the road for you. All you have to do is learn how to spot a good real estate investment and use your equity from another property to cover the purchasing costs and use financing to cover the rest.

Understand the market

The first step you have to take to understand the real estate market where you are investing is to study and understand the real estate market in the area where you are considering buying. It is not only about what types of properties are selling well in the area, but also about what types of properties lenders are interested in financing.

You can get an idea of what the ideal loan is by shopping around and talking to the loan officers or originators. Find out from the loan officers which types of properties the lender has been financing the most lately. You should also ask them which types of properties have the most attractive interest rates and financing terms. The more interested a lender is in financing a particular property type, the more beneficial the terms and conditions are going to be. For example, a lender may be more interested in financing the purchase of a flagship hotel (i.e., Hilton or Marriott) than he or she is in financing a warehouse or office condos according to the lender's preferences. The types of properties a lender will finance has a lot to do with secondary marketing, which is the market where lenders sell their loans. If lenders are not able to sell their loans in the secondary market, then they may not be interested in financing it in the first place. Whether lenders sell their mortgages on the secondary market or not, they may only be interested in financing the types of properties that are the most lucrative for them. Having a conversation with a loan officer or representative for the lender can help to point you in the direction of the types of properties they are interested in financing, which means it will be much easier for you to get approved for the loan as well.

Once you determine the property types that lenders are interested in financing, you have to consider how much cash flow these property types can bring you. The best way to determine the cash flow of the property is to have a professional accountant review the financial books for an existing building or property, which can be obtained for the current owner. You also have to take into consideration how the financing affects your cash flow and ultimately the profit you bring in, which is where a tax advisor comes in. A tax advisor can help you determine the after-tax basis for owing and operating the building and whether it financially benefits you.

Buy what you know

Similar to starting a business based on your skills or interests, buying the type(s) of real estate you know, understand, or have experience with can also prove to be more beneficial to you and your wallet. At a 2009 seminar, a millionaire investor speaking to the audience described an investment he made in a vegetable processing plant. He spent $1 million to buy the property and the business, which sent him into bankruptcy a few months later.

Why? He did not know anything about running this type of business.

The same concept holds true when you are considering real estate property types for investment purposes. It is not about buying the same types of property that other investors in the community are buying; it is about investing in a property that you feel comfortable in buying, owning, and possibly operating, depending on the type of property. This may mean buying in your local community because that is where you live and work; you are most familiar with the area, its zoning and building codes, and what is happening in the local real estate market. This provides you with a better chance to succeed at your first real estate investment and gives you a foundation to build on – possibly for buying your future real estate investments.

The Pros and Cons of Each Type of Property

It is a reality that there are investors who make money with every type of real estate property they invest in. On the other hand, there are investors who lose money on every type of property they invest in. Beyond your knowledge of the investment property type, it is also important to note that the location of the property plays a big role in how profitable it can be. Nothing illustrates this point better than the real estate downturn that started in 2007. Some of the hardest hit areas included Florida, California, and Michigan. These are also the same three areas that saw the biggest spike in real estate values prior to that downturn. These markets were hot locations to buy property because investors knew that they could sell it for a profit at a later date, but when the real estate market tanked, it was at an even higher rate than other areas in the country. So although property type can determine how much money you can generate in income on a monthly basis or profit from when you sell it, the location of the property you invest in is just as important a factor to consider.

The question still remains: Which type of property is the best investment option for you? Learning about the pros and cons of each type of investment property permits you to get a better grasp on which one best fits your financial goals and investment options.

Rental apartments

Rental apartment investments range from owning one unit to owning an entire complex. Almost every community in the country has apartment rentals, but the best apartment rentals for investment purposes are in areas where the population consists of middle-income individuals and families. This demographic makes enough money to pay for rent, but not quite enough to buy their own apartment or home. While this is the ideal situation for owning apartment rentals, it is not the only one that is beneficial. Other areas where owning rental apartments or properties can be beneficial are in college towns or in areas where there is a high concentration of individuals or couples in their early 20s. These demographic groups are typically more inclined to rent than to buy because of a lower annual income.

The most beneficial aspect of owning apartment rentals is the future possibility of converting the units into condos (a.k.a, a condo conversion). It happened in Miami Beach in the late 1990s: Real estate developers and investors were scooping up rental apartment buildings — high rises and smaller complexes. While some buildings were completely gutted and rebuilt, others were renovated or kept exactly the same. After the condo conversion, units were sold for hundreds of thousands of dollars as compared to the meager monthly rental amounts typically running between $700 and $1,000 per month, depending on the size of the apartment. Remember that in a condo conversion situation, the units you are converting were rented out before the renovations and conversion. A condo conversion involves turning rental apartments into condos that are then sold as individual condo units.

One of the best ways to get started in investing in the apartment rental market is to live in one of the units while you rent out the others you own. This is especially true if you do not currently own a home, but rent instead. It creates a kill-two-birds-with-one-stone scenario because you stop throwing away your money on renting and start building equity in your own apartment — the unit where you are living — while taking advantage of the income investment rental apartments can produce.

While apartment rentals are considered one of the best real estate investments, there are also some drawbacks to ownership. If you choose to manage the property yourself rather than hire a professional management company, you may find running and operating the complex takes up a lot of your time. If running the complex is not your full-time job, then this may be a problem.

There are also instances where you have non-paying tenants and have to go through the eviction process, which is another time-wasting and money-sucking venture. Then there are maintenance costs for upkeep on the property, such as the landscaping, pool, clubhouse, and fitness center; while some of these amenities may be optional, they are quickly becoming a standard in most apartment rentals, making it nearly impossible for a rental lacking these facilities to flourish. So while you consider the good in owning apartment rental, it is also important to weigh the disadvantages that may affect your profit.

Commercial rentals

Similar to residential rentals are commercial rentals. Commercial rentals can vary from strip mall shopping centers and large malls to office buildings and complexes. In comparing residential rentals to commercial rentals, the lease agreements with residential tenants are usually shorter than commercial tenants. Commercial tenants tend to stay in one place longer than residential ones, so your income potential is safer and has a longer term. Commercial leases tend to run between five and ten years rather than one-year leases you see in rental apartments or residential rental properties (single-family homes, duplexes, and multiplexes). Generally speaking, the monthly rate charged for a commercial lease is also higher than a residential lease, so commercial rentals tend to afford you more income on a monthly basis. On the other hand, running a commercial property can be more expensive than a residential property because of the cost of electricity, maintenance of the building, landscaping, and common areas of the property.

The first disadvantage to commercial rentals is it usually takes more staff to run and operate it. These types of rentals consume more of your time than residential units and can eat up more of your money, too. The second major disadvantage is that commercial rentals typically do not have a conversion option built in, so you will not have developers and real estate investors beating down your door to buy the property or the option of converting and selling the individual units yourself. There are some exceptions to this, so you may have an opportunity to sell the individual units to current tenants or new business tenants at some point.

Condotels

Condotels – condo hotels – are unique types of property. The individual condo units are sold to individual owners. When the individual owners are not occupying the unit, it is rented out and maintained for them. You, as the owner of the condotel, operate it as a hotel. Rather than normal hotel rooms, the units are typically condos or suite-like rooms with a kitchen, bedroom(s), main area, and bathroom(s). While others own the individual units, you rent these units out to the people who need a place to stay, so it is like renting a room from a hotel. There is a front desk where guests check in and out, and a maid service that cleans and refreshes the units for each guest as the condo is turned over.

The main benefit to owning this type of property is it has the potential to be turned into or converted into timeshares or vacation rentals. If your condotel is located in an area that benefits from tourism, it can be a huge moneymaker. As the condotel owner, you can sell fairly easily and walk away with a profit. For example, owning a condotel in some of the major ski locations such as Vermont or Colorado, lakeside condotels in the Midwest, or beachside locations in Florida and South Carolina can prove to be lucrative investments. Owning a condotel near major family attractions such as Walt Disney World Resort in Orlando, Florida, or Disneyland Resort in California are two additional vacation spots where condotels have a chance to thrive.

Properties you can convert

There is a common thread in finding a property in which to invest: If you can find a property that is selling below market value and can turn it into a property that you can then sell above the current price, this is the best type of real estate investment to make. A conversion is a change in the purpose or use of the property as it currently stands; for example, you could buy a motel at a depressed market value and turn it into a retirement home. It is important that you understand what types of properties are bringing in more value — such as retirement homes — and the properties that are most like it to minimize the cost of the conversion. There also has to be a demand for the property you are converting.

The key to profiting from this type of conversion is an in-depth knowledge of the real estate market where the property is located. You need to know and understand what types of properties are economically disadvantaged so you can buy at bargain pricing; then, you need to know how to convert into a more lucrative property type – whether you sell or manage it. Knowledge of the local zoning and building codes are also imperative because these laws and regulations can determine what you can and cannot use the property for. Your best source for finding out this information is from the building and zoning department in the county where you are considering investing. You can also speak with real estate agents and attorneys, as they are good resources of information on the real estate climate in the area.

Hotels and motels

Another way to invest your money for profit is in buying hotels or motels. One advantage to this type of property is that depending on its size, it takes a lot of staff to run a hotel. This may create a new career opportunity for you, your friends, and your family to run and manage the facility. Whether you run the hotel using your family as staff or you hire third-party staff members, you have to pay employment fees. At least if you and your family are running the hotel, then you are reaping the income benefits, so it is like paying yourself. It also brings you profit from renting out each room time after time. It is one of the routes to earning the greatest amount of wealth, which may explain why millionaires are drawn to investing in hotels. One of the other ways you can profit from a hotel or motel was discussed earlier. You can convert it into a timeshare, vacation rental, or sell the property outright to a developer. Owning, operating, and selling these types of properties can bring you a significant amount of wealth, but there are drawbacks to owning hotels and motels, too.

Hotel and motel operations can be difficult to manage. For the most part, if you are interested in buying and investing in these types of properties, you need to either manage it yourself or hire someone you can count on to run it for you. By being in control of the daily operations, you will help to ensure that the hotel remains profitable.

Industrial buildings

While it can be one of the most lucrative forms of investment properties, zoning for industrial buildings is one of the hardest to find. There are certain areas of most towns and cities zoned specifically for industrial use, but there are some areas across the country where you will not find any industrial buildings within the city limits because the residents of the town or city vote not to allow these types of buildings to be built in the area. Zoning and building notices must be sent to the residents of the town or area before a new structure can be built. A meeting must take place where the residents have an opportunity to voice their opinions before the zoning and building board make its vote. While the residents do not always keep these types of properties from being built in their town, it sometimes sways the board to vote against allowing certain types of buildings to be built.

The biggest advantage of owning an industrial property is that the tenants typically pay all of the expenses, which means a lot more money ends up in your pocket than with the other types of buildings and real estate properties. Expenses covered by industrial building tenants include the cost for property taxes, insurance, maintenance, and upkeep on the building. This is on top of the rent they pay to occupy the building. It depends on the terms and conditions that are spelled out in the lease agreement between you and the tenant, but generally an industrial tenant pays the rent directly to you, and the tenant pays all of the rest of the expenses to the appropriate parties. This type of lease is referred to as a triple net lease (NNN).

One of the disadvantages is that an industrial tenant can leave at any time, and because there is only one tenant in the building, you may not find out about their departure for quite some time. This is why it is important for you to thoroughly check the credit and references of an industrial tenant to find out what their rental history is — whether they made lease payments on time, if they have ever broken a lease before, or damaged the properties where they previously rented. Checking with previous landlords and seeing if there are any collections on their credit related to property rental is one way to ensure you are renting to property to a reliable tenant. This is true of any type of tenant — industrial or residential — but the difference is that industrial tenants have more expenses involved in renting the building. These extra expenses may become overwhelming for industrial tenants and lead them to abandon the building. For example, as the building ages, items become outdated and may cost too much for the tenant to fix or upkeep. So rather than fixing or updating these items, they skip out on the lease and leave you hanging. Because industrial properties have many idiosyncrasies, they are not recommended for those new to real estate investing.

Single-family homes

One of the most common real estate investments is the purchase of a single-family home, which is typically purchased as the primary residence for the owner to live in. These properties still offer a good return on your investment, depending on several variables. If you buy a home, live in it for some time, then sell it for a higher amount than you paid for it, or for more than what you owe on any outstanding mortgage or equity line, you will profit from the sale.

Many real estate investors purchase a single-family home to live in and rent it out when they move to another home. These savvy investors use the equity they have built up in this primary residence to fund the purchase of their new home, so they do not have to come up with any money to cover down payments and closing costs on the new purchase. On top of this, they rent their old home out for more than their monthly obligations on the property, so they walk away with a monthly income as well. So now the investor owns two pieces of real estate, and the renter is paying for one of them. Depending on the amount of money you have left from the rent payment after covering all of the other costs of the property, the rent payment you are charging may leave you enough left over to cover some or all of the expenses on the new home you bought (and are currently living in).

The flip side of owning a single-family home is that it can be expensive. Any and all maintenance costs fall on your shoulders. Air conditioning and heating units, plumbing, roof repairs and replacements, and real estate taxes are only a few of the very expensive items required for upkeep on houses. When you rent a home or apartment, the landlord is responsible for these costs, and you are only responsible for paying the rent. Then, there is the matter of homeowner's insurance, which has tripled in some areas recently because of natural disasters and catastrophes. In some cases, the rising cost of homeowner's insurance has created a situation in which homeowners are no longer able to afford owning their homes with the proper amount of insurance coverage. For example, during the 2005 hurricane season when Florida was pummeled with five hurricanes (one of which was Katrina), Florida homeowners saw such an increase in homeowner's insurance premiums that some were forced to sell their homes because they could no longer afford the insurance. You may think it is as easy as dropping the amount of insurance coverage on the home, but when you have a mortgage on the property, a lender requires you to have a certain type of coverage and carry a certain amount on the property because of the lien.

Even with all of the added expenses of owning a home, single-family homes can be great investment opportunities. Bottom-dollar sales prices, like those seen during the 2007-2008 housing crisis, indicate the perfect time to scoop up homes and rent them out. But when home prices are level, there is still an opportunity to make money on owning single-family homes as a long-term investment strategy.

In order to maximize the return on your investment, you want to look for areas that have high employment rates and where older homes are selling right along with new homes. You also want to buy in desirable neighborhoods where you — and ultimately the buyer or renter — want to live, such as neighborhoods with low crime and low traffic.

Timeshares

Earlier in this chapter, we talked about the conversion option of turning a hotel, motel, or condotel into a timeshare. Because there are several different types of timeshares, it is important to understand the differences to determine which one may bring you the greatest return on your investment. A timeshare owner who holds a warranty deed on the unit has access to the unit for a week at a specific time of the year. The timeframe is spelled out as to the specific period that the buyer's week starts and ends, and it is applied year after year as long as the buyer still owns the property. Floating-time timeshares, however, do not specify the time period that the buyer has access to the property, but it still entitles the buyer to access to the unit for one week during the year. Each timeshare has its own way of assigning the week that each buyer has access to the unit.

Points systems are another form of owning a timeshare, which is where the buyer does not own a specific unit, but is assigned a set of points that gives them access to a unit in the timeshare. This works similarly to a credit card reward program where you earn points as you make purchases and cash these points in for prizes. In this case, instead of cashing the points in for prizes, you are redeeming your points for the use a timeshare unit. So depending on when you choose to exercise your points, one or more of the units in the building may be available for you to use, but it may not be the same unit year after year, as it is when you own a warranty deed or floating timeshare.

Then there are fractional-ownership timeshares, which differ in a couple of different ways from your average timeshare. First, fractional-ownership timeshares are not limited to one property; the company you purchase the timeshare from owns different properties where you can apply your ownership. Second, it is not limited to one week per year but can run from intervals of one to three months instead.

The final type of timeshare is a vacation club, which requires a much larger upfront investment, often more than $100,000. Your "club membership" gives you access to a variety of properties. Some of these properties are located in foreign and exotic locations, while others are domestic properties. This is a big, money-making business. If you own a hotel that you convert into a condotel and eventually into a vacation club, you stand to make a lot of money on your investment. Not only do vacation club members have to pay the large, upfront fee to own one of the units, but they are also responsible for paying an annual membership fee and a portion of the maintenance and management fees.

One of the advantages to owning or investing in a timeshare is you obtain full rights to the property, including the title. In the event of your death, your heirs or beneficiaries can inherit the property. When you own an individual timeshare unit, then you have the benefit to use the timeshare at a fraction of what it would cost you to buy and maintain a vacation condo or home that is not in use for most of the year.

If you are the owner of the entire timeshare complex, this can be a very lucrative arrangement for you. You can sell the individual units to timeshare buyers many times over, and you receive a payment from each investor. If each timeshare buyer has access to the unit for one week each year and there are 52 weeks in the year, this means that you are receiving 52 payments each year on one unit. Consider if your timeshare has 100 units and the timeshares investment amount for each timeshare buyer is $10,000. Then, income from owning the timeshare complex looks something like this:

Number of payments X Number of units = Payments received per year

52 X 100 = 5,200

Cost of each timeshare X Payments received each year = Total annual income

$10,000 X 5,200 = $52,000,000

Vacant land

The final real estate investment option you can purchase in an effort to bring you a return on your investment is vacant land, which is raw land that does not have a home or some other type of building on it.

There are two ways you can profit from investing in raw land. If you have an immediate use for the property, you start to see the return on your investment more quickly by planning to turn the raw land into a usable property by building a hotel, home, or some other type of property on it in the near future. The second option to profit from vacant land is to buy land with the intent to have it zoned or converted for a higher economic purpose. This works best when you buy land in an up-and-coming area where progress is coming but has not quite been finalized. For example, a tile store business owner bought 67 acres of land zoned for agriculture. Before he bought the land, he fully researched the area and studied local zoning and government codes. He found out the property could be zoned for residential purposes and applied for the rezoning as soon as he purchased the property. Five years later, he sold this property to a housing developer for a profit. The developer divided up the 67 acres into 67, one-acre lots that he built single-family homes on that sold for approximately $1 million each. If the property had remained zoned as agricultural property, it may never have attracted the windfall as the property did zoned residentially.

The disadvantage of buying vacant land is that it can take a long time for you to see a return on your investment. In the previous example, it took the owner of the land five years to see a return on his investment. In some instances it takes even longer. There are also many variables that affect the return on your investment, including the progression of the area and how this affects property values. Changes in the local government toward development and zoning ordinance changes are two other factors that can have a positive or negative impact on the value of the land over time and how much you can profit from the sale or use of it.

For example, if you buy a property with the intention to build a commercial property on it but the zoning ordinances change, it can prevent you from using the land as you originally intended. On the other hand, if you own a residential home on a main street, and zoning changes turn it into commercial-use property, you can now rent the property out or sell it to a business entity. You have probably noticed that some business locations look like residential homes; this is because it was a residential home, and either the owner requested a zoning change for the building, or the local government voted in a zoning change for the area where the property was located.

The Big Picture

The entire premise of this book is to share how you can leverage the equity you have built in an existing property to make additional money in another investment. This chapter is about how to leverage the equity in a property you own to use for the down payment or closing costs on the purchase of another piece of real estate. The rest of the money for the purchase of the new property comes from financing by a bank or mortgage lender. Not only are you leveraging the equity in your own real estate, but you are also leveraging the bank's money to put more money in your pocket.

The key to maximizing your return on the equity in a property and other people's money is to create the most beneficial financing option. You want to create a situation where you maximize the cash flow of the property, maximize the equity buildup of the property, or both. The great news is that there are many ways to structure each of your real estate transactions to help you achieve one of these goals.

For example, say you have your eye on a ten-unit apartment complex for sale for $500,000. It is located in an up-and-coming area of downtown near the business district. You are interested in it because you envision remodeling each of the ten units to attract the young professionals who work nearby. You have a $250,000 equity line, so you have the ability to write a check for $250,000 of the purchase price and finance the other 50 percent through a bank. Before you do that, though, it is also important to think about how much it will cost you to remodel the units. If you can do most of the work yourself, and you have a friend who is a general contractor, you determine that the cost for remodeling all ten units will cost you approximately $250,000.

This changes everything because the $250,000 you once had for a 50 percent down payment is now needed to cover the remodeling cost. Remember, the purpose of remodeling the units is to attract a higher-caliber tenant who is willing to pay a higher rent. Now, depending on your goal, there are a couple of different ways you can structure the purchase and remodeling of the building. If you want to maximize the return on your cash flow, then your deal may look something like this:

Rent from 10 units ($1,200/month for 12 months)	$144,000
Less operating expenses (40 percent of gross rent)	- $57,600
Net operating income	$86,400
100% financing (7% interest via mortgage calculator)	- $34,992
Cash flow before taxes	$51,408

This offers you the maximum cash flow on the property because you have zero money (none of your equity funds) invested in the property, and you are still walking away with $51,408 a year on the property. The scenario would look different if your goal is to maximize the equity buildup in the property. After doing your homework, you discover that condo units are selling for $300 per square foot. You still have to remodel the units, but instead of renting them out to create monthly cash flow, you can sell each unit for a profit — even after figuring in the remodeling costs.

For example, if each unit is 1,200 square feet, then with ten units, you have 12,000 square feet for sale. At $300 per square foot, you can sell out the entire complex for a gross sale of $3.6 million. For the condo conversion, the profit situation breaks down like this:

Potential gross sales	$3,600,000
Less purchase price	- $500,000
Less remodeling costs	- $250,000
Less marketing costs	- $50,000
Less loan interest paid during remodeling	- $35,000
Total profit	$2,765,000

With the rental option, in one year you walk away with a little more than $50,000 per year. With the condo conversion option, you walk away with $200,000 in profit when you sell all of the units, which would take you approximately four years to reach if you chose the rental option. But because of the high reward, the condo conversion option has more risk associated with it than keeping the building as rental apartments.

There is risk associated with any real estate transaction, whether it is buying a single-family home you plan on living in or buying an apartment complex you rent out to tenants. The riskier the investment, the more earning potential it has. You can, however, lose the principal you use to invest in the property, as well as any other costs involved in running and maintaining the property. Real estate investment successes or failures depend mostly on the current real estate market situation, which includes the supply and demand of properties and how much tenants and buyers of the properties are willing to pay. In situations where the real estate market is depressed, you may be forced sell for a lower price than you paid for the property, or to hold on to the property to avoid taking a loss on your investment.

CASE STUDY: FLIPPING HOMES TO FLIP A PROFIT

Kim Adamof
Realtor
www.Realtor.com

Although Kim Adamof and her husband, John, made some mistakes using the equity in their home to invest in other pieces of real estate, they have also walked away with profits. In 2004, the Adamofs attended a real estate investment meeting where a "rehab queen" spoke on flipping houses. They listened to what she had to say and started to get excited. The last home they had owned in Pennsylvania was a fixer-upper, and they walked away from the sale of this home with the profit in their pocket.

When they moved to North Carolina, they used all of the money from the sale of the Pennsylvania home to purchase their new home. This meant they had a lot of equity built in the North Carolina property. For Adamof, this equity was like a security blanket; she felt safe knowing she was sitting on a pile of money — even if it was tied up in her home.

One thing that the rehab queen said that stuck with the Adamofs was that they should obtain their real estate licenses, and so they did. From the same meeting, they had met a mortgage broker who tried to convince them to access the equity they had built in their home to fund a new house-flipping business. Adamof felt her security blanket was in jeopardy, so she did not refinance her home at the time to pull the equity out of it.

After Adamof became a Realtor, she listed a home that needed a lot of repairs. She saw an opportunity to buy the home herself, make the repairs, and sell it for a profit. She convinced her husband this is what they should do. After all, she had gotten into the real estate business to be a "flipper," and she had not bought anything yet.

The Adamofs obtained a home equity line of credit on their home through a local bank. With the line of credit for $100,000, they purchased the home with cash from their equity line. Because of their previous experience with their home in Pennsylvania, they were confident they would walk away with a profit from the sale of this home as well.

They hired a contractor to make the repairs needed on the home. Because of a delay with the repairs and unforeseen wood rot on the bottom of the house, they have been trying to unload the house since October 2007. They currently have the house under contract, but the buyer wants the wood rot repaired before closing on the sale. Overall, the Adamofs stand to lose $30,000 on this deal.

They learned a valuable lesson from this experience — use your line of credit for the down payment and to cover closing costs. Finance the rest of the purchase with a mortgage or with a private investor. Adamof took what she learned from her first mistake of purchasing the home with the entire equity line and went on to find her next house-flipping deal.

A few months after she bought her first house to be flipped, Adamof listed another property for sale that belonged to a couple going through a divorce who were behind on their mortgage payments. An investor Adamof knew suggested that she short-sale the home.

Because she did not have any cash on hand, as it was tied up in the original home she bought, she contacted one of her past clients who was interested in investing some of his money in real estate. Using 90 percent of her client's money and 10 percent from her home equity line, Adamof bought the home, had all the repairs done, and sold it three months later for a $30,000 profit. She split the proceeds with her investor 50/50, so she walked away with $15,000 in profit.

Spotting properties with potential for more cash flow

So, if your goal is to maximize your cash flow, there are techniques to help you learn to spot properties that have the potential to earn you the cash flow you are looking for to reach your goal. This is true whether you plan to maintain the current use of the property or convert the building for a more economically advantaged purpose.

Five characteristics of properties with potential

1. **Properties under poor management**: These properties need some attention and the right management to turn them around. Right now, the property sits in a good area and has the potential to earn more in rent with a more hands-on management style and with basic upkeep of the property. Cleaning up the trash, maintaining the landscaping, and creating a better environment will also attract a higher caliber of tenants – tenants who can and will pay more in rent.

2. **Properties with below-market rents**: Because you have done your homework and researched the area you are considering purchasing the property in, you know that the rental rate currently being charged is below market value. The key to fixing the problem that is causing the rental rates before market value is to figure out what the problem is. Is it poor management? Is it the caliber of tenants? Is it both? Once you find out what is holding the property back from its earning potential, you can correct the problem and increase the rental rate.

3. **Increased rental rates with simple and inexpensive improvements**: Changing the look and feel of an apartment complex or commercial office complex easily change the rent amounts. Proper assessment of the property before you buy it and proper planning in implementing the changes in the right timeframe is essential.

4. **The property is located in an up-and-coming area**: Positive upcoming changes to an area typically impact the

property values positively as well. Generally, this occurs when new infrastructure is introduced to the area. This type of cash flow increase potential tends to have a delayed effect, though, because you cannot increase rent rates until the infrastructure changes are complete. Because new roadways and other infrastructure changes can take years to finish, you may own the property for several years before you realize the increased cash flow.

5. **Conversion for economic advantage**: Infrastructure changes also create a potential for converting the building's purpose to bring in more cash flow. This is especially true as construction costs continue to rise, which makes converting an existing building much cheaper than having to build a property from scratch.

It is possible to use the existing equity you have in a property to buy another piece of real estate and profit from it. Combining the use of your equity funds with creative financing helps to maximize your cash flow, maximize your profit, or both. How you approach it is up to you, your willingness to take risk, and the upfront work you do to make sure you know what you are doing before you purchase the property.

Buying a New Primary Residence

Though many homeowners sell one home or primary residence before buying another one, others leverage the equity in their current home for the down payment and closing costs of buying a new home. This is probably one of the most common and easiest ways to use the equity in your current primary residence to buy real estate. There are some setbacks that can occur, but using the equity in a current home to buy a new one puts you in a position where you can buy a new home without having to sell your existing one first.

One catch is that you usually cannot have your current home on the market in order to take out a new equity line or to do a cash-out refinance. Many lenders will not allow you to tap into the equity or take out a new mortgage on a property that you intend on selling in the near future. There are a couple of different reasons lenders feel this way:

1. Lenders do not want to lend you short-term money to buy another piece of property because once you use their money to buy your other property, you are going to sell the property (which is the collateral for the loan). Lenders essentially lose out on the deal because they are not going to really earn much — or very little — interest on the deal.

2. This type of short-term financing is considered to be a bridge loan — bridging the time between you buying your new property and selling the existing property — which is a type of loan that is hard to sell on the secondary market because it does not bring investors a big rate of return. This means that the lender has to shelve the loan, and it sits on his or her books instead of being sold. Essentially, it messes up the balance sheet of the lender and makes it look as though they are not profitable.

This points out another advantage to setting up an equity line, even if you do not have an immediate need to use it. Situations where you need access to short-term funds allow you to use the existing equity line to put a cash down payment and cover the closing costs of buying a new home in the future without having to rely on the profits from the sale of the existing home.

The other detail you have to keep in mind is that you have to be able to carry two house payments until the old home sells or rents. If the only mortgage you have on the property is the equity line, then your costs may be minimal, making it easier to keep up the payments on two homes at once. If you have a mortgage on the old home and a mortgage on the new home, then you will find yourself in a situation where you have two mortgage payments (and possibly an equity line payment) until you are able to sell the original home.

This is another real estate purchase situation where you want to use a combination of the equity in your existing home and financing on the new home to create the best financial outcome. The equity line or equity funds act as a cushion for you to accomplish the purchase of the new home. Without access to these funds, you may have to put your existing home up for sale and wait until it sells in order to use the proceeds from the sale to buy a new home.

Some lenders do offer equity lines on a home you intend on selling. This short-term financing option is referred to as a bridge loan because it "bridges" the transition from the old home to the new home until you can sell your old home. With more stringent lending guidelines in place, bridge loans are harder to obtain.

Leveraging your first home to buy another single-family home is one of the most popular ways for a new real estate investor to become an expert. You buy your first home, live it in for a while, and use that equity to buy a new home. Then, you rent out your old home while living in your new home. You can then use the equity in one or both of the properties you now own to buy a new home. This time, have your sights on a duplex, where you plan on living in one unit and renting out the other. Now you are collecting three rents: two from the two single-family homes you are renting out, and one rent payment from the tenants living in the other side of the duplex while you live on the other side of the duplex. This behavior allows you to ease your way into being a real estate investor. It makes it easier for you to continue buying single-family homes or duplexes, or it can lead to the opportunity to experience the ownership of other types of real estate.

Multiple-rental property management

There are some of the same concerns in owning several single-family homes or duplexes as there are in owning and operating multiple apartment complexes or commercial rentals.

Managing multiple investment properties can be a lucrative way to invest your money, but it can also be trying. First, you have to have the ability to multitask. Each property has its own characteristics, problems, and issues that make it unique. Flexibility is a must when managing multiple properties. You may be dealing with putting in new carpet in one office building, then turn around and have to announce to the tenants of a condo that the rent is increasing when their leases are renewed. It is similar to running several different companies at the same time. Real estate investors who own multiple properties typically do it as a full-time business that they manage themselves, or they hire property managers to handle the day-to-day operations of each property. Regardless of how many you own, you still have to maintain the property, and the more properties you own, the more you will have to maintain.

Regardless of the type of the real estate you choose to invest in, there are opportunities to create cash flow or turn a profit. It is all about the approach you take to leverage the equity and financing options available to create the best possible outcome.

Checklist	
✓	Decide what your goal is in investing your equity funds in real estate
✓	Weigh the options of increasing monthly cash flow or maximizing profit earnings
✓	Research the real estate market in the area you are considering purchasing in
✓	Decide if you are able to run or own the type of property you are buying
✓	Beyond the purchase price and mortgage payments, determine the other costs involved in running, operating, and maintaining the property
✓	Calculate your profit or cash flow after the debts and expenses are backed out
✓	Determine if the profit or cash flow is worth making the investment

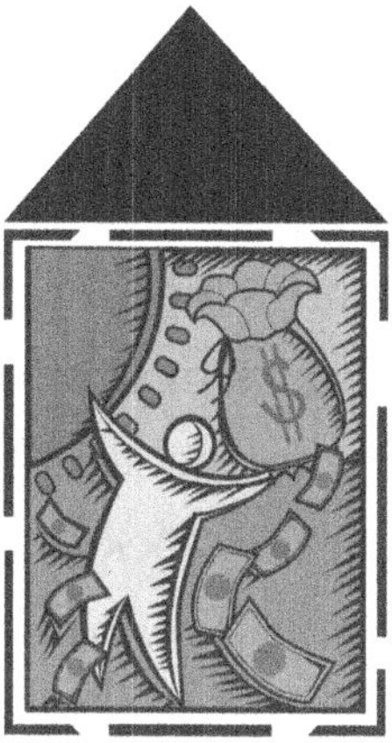

CHAPTER 8

Private Mortgages

In this chapter you will:

- Learn the definition of a private mortgage
- Discover how you can invest your equity funds in private mortgages
- Calculate the possible return on your investment in private mortgages
- Uncover how the private mortgage investment works and where you can find these investments
- Understand the risks involved with investing in private mortgages
- Discover what type of individuals seek private mortgages

Because you know what a mortgage is, you can probably figure out that a private mortgage is between the deed holder and the buyer, rather than the buyer and the bank. Private mortgages also go by other names, such as trust deeds and hard-money lending. Whatever name you call it, private mortgages are short-term loans made to real estate purchasers that use the property as collateral to secure the loan. At this point, you may be wondering how you can actually make money by lending money to others.

Investors who invest their money in private mortgages can see a return in their investment at a rate of 12, 15, and even 18 percent. This is a higher rate of return than many stocks or mutual fund investments provide. Investing in private mortgages also involves lower risk than investing your money in the stock market. Finally, private mortgage investments pay you a return on your money on a monthly basis, so you do not have to wait to start seeing your return.

This means you can create a better quality of life for you and your family without much of a threat to your principal investment. It is also a great tool for building wealth or a larger nest egg in a shorter period of time.

How it Works

There are two main ways you can invest in private mortgages – create the mortgage note yourself or buy the note through a professional hard-money lending institution. No matter which option you choose, it is important to understand that investing in private mortgages is a contractually binding agreement between you and the borrower. In essence, you are acting as a bank or mortgage lender because it is your money that is funding the loan. The buyer or owner of the property is the borrower and the deed holder. When you lend your money to a private borrower, the loan is also secured by the property itself. In essence, the property is collateral for the mortgage, which provides a safety net for your investment. You also receive monthly payments from the borrower based on the terms of the promissory note that both parties sign and agree to abide by when the loan is established.

When you sell your own property and hold the mortgage on the property for the buyer, this is known as seller financing. You are the mortgage lender, instead of the buyer obtaining financing from a bank or third-party lending institution. Only about 10 percent of buyers and sellers enter into a seller financing agreement, but it is an increasingly popular way to sell property faster and easier when lending guidelines are strict or there is a faltering housing or lending market, where it may be hard to obtain traditional financing, or where the buyer is looking for a quick turnaround time for closing the deal.

Because this is a property you own, you would sell it for the going rate in the market and require the buyer to put some amount in the form of a cash down payment to show good faith – be it $1,000 or $10,000. Then, you would have a promissory note drawn up by a legal professional to ensure repayment of the note. Not only do you receive principal payments, but you also receive interest on that principal. Keep in mind that this is interest on money that is sitting in the value of your real estate, not money that has come out of your pocket or your equity line. If you have a mortgage on the property, this option may not work for you because the lender with an existing lien on the property has to approve additional liens that may affect their being paid off in case of default. If you own the home free and clear, then private mortgages will put your equity to work.

Another way to create your own mortgage note is to seek out real estate investors who are seeking private lending. The challenge is in finding a professional real estate investor with good credit and payment history. It is possible to find these investors by placing classified ads in local real estate publications and online or by networking with investors at local real estate investment clubs and condominium associations. As you become involved in private money lending, you will also obtain referrals for qualified real estate investors interested in your investment.

It is important to be very careful and to put the time and effort into evaluating the borrowers' ability to repay the loan (also known as due diligence). You are also going to need some real estate legal assistance to complete the transaction. Although there are standard agreements and deeds you can use for these transactions, you do not want to put your money at risk over a legal technicality. Spend the extra money for a professional real estate attorney to draw up these documents and make sure everything is in proper order.

Private mortgages, where a seller is financing the mortgage for the borrower, typically have a term of five years or fewer. The mortgage payments are amortized over a 30-year period, but at the end of the five years, the note becomes due — to you — so the borrower has to pay the remaining balance or refinance with a more traditional lender. If you do not currently own the property but wish to invest in private mortgages, there are private mortgage companies and hard moneylenders that can help you invest.

The other primary option for you to invest in private mortgages is through a hard-money lender or private mortgage broker, especially if you are new to this type of investment, as they can save you time and money. These professionals act as matchmakers between investors and individuals looking for private money funds. You can find a list of private moneylenders and brokers online using your favorite search engine. Talk with and compare at least three of these companies before deciding which one you feel the most comfortable with. You will want to compare the fees, interest rate, and the terms for each mortgage offered by the private money lender — just as you would do if you were comparing traditional mortgages between lenders — to see which option is the most financially beneficial to you and your financial situation.

The main advantage of working with these professionals is you do not have to find the borrower yourself. Private moneylenders and mortgage brokers have a pool of clients they are working with. Second, these private moneylenders do all of the background and credit checks on the borrowers to ensure that they are creditworthy, which increases your chances of earning a greater return on your investment and decreases the chances the borrower will default on the loan. Finally, private money brokers and lenders process all of the legal paperwork and documents necessary for the mortgage.

Brokers also provide the servicing of the loan after it is funded, so they deal with the payment collection, keep payment records, and track the balance due. If the borrower defaults on the loan, the broker also handles the collection calls, letters, and paperwork involved. Finally, if the loan goes into foreclosure, the broker processes the paperwork and proceeds with the foreclosure process on your behalf.

There are also some cases where the broker will find a new investor to buy your note if, for some reason, you no longer wish to hold the mortgage. Because the lender or broker plays such a vital role in your investment, it is imperative that you feel comfortable working with the broker and that you feel he or she has your best interests aligned with his or her best interests.

You will pay a small fee for the broker, but you benefit from his or her experience. Ultimately, this also increases the return on your investment. Typically, the broker charges 4 to 8 points – or percent – of the loan to originate, process, and service the loan between you and the borrower. For example, if the amount you are lending is $50,000, and the broker charges 4 points, then the fee paid to the broker is $2,000. The fee you pay to the broker does not affect the yield you receive on your investment. According to the terms and conditions of the mortgage agreement, if the interest rate charged to the borrower is 12 percent, then your yield remains 12 percent, regardless of the fee you pay to the broker.

Why Seller Financing or Private Mortgage Investment?

The biggest advantage to investing in private mortgages is the high yield of return it can provide. The borrowers in these situations are willing to pay a premium, which equates to a higher interest rate than the market value, because they need a short-term loan and want to avoid – or cannot qualify for – financing a purchase or refinance with a bank or mortgage lender.

Borrowers who do not qualify for traditional financing with lower interest rates and better terms typically have some credit problems or liens against the property that prohibit them from qualifying. Other times, it is the property that prohibits the borrower from financing it. If the property is located in an area outside of conventional financing guidelines, or the loan amount is too small for the lender, then seller financing or private mortgage lending may be the borrower's only option. Some lenders will not lend in certain areas — areas that are too rural or do not meet certain standards or guidelines the lender follows. For example, a military retiree and his wife bought 72 acres of land in the western part of Tennessee. Even with perfect credit, the only financing they could obtain was from the local bank in the town where the property was located. Other lenders would not even consider financing it because it was too much property and located in too rural of an area.

As the private mortgage investor, you are protected — in the case of default — by the property that secures the promissory note between you and the borrower. These types of mortgages also have a lower loan-to-value (LTV) ratio than bank and mortgage lender loans. An approved and experienced appraiser determines the value of the property. The amount of financing is then determined by a percentage (set by the lender) of the appraised value. This loan amount percentage is known as a loan-to-value ratio. For single-family homes, LTVs are usually 70 percent or less, while apartments and condominiums, as well as commercial and industrial properties, have LTVs of 65 percent or less.

Home price X LTV = Maximum amount of financing
$100,000 X .70 = $70,000

Types of properties

Private mortgages are funded on various types of properties. The four main categories of properties that use private money lending are residential, commercial, agricultural, and industrial. Properties that fall under these four main categories include private homes, duplexes, apartment complexes, office buildings, working farms, and more. The terms and conditions of a private mortgage are negotiated between you as the private mortgage investor and the borrower, unless you are working with a broker. A broker would negotiate these terms on your behalf. So whether you are funding a commercial or residential property, it is up to you what interest rate, term, and payments you require from the borrower.

No matter what type of property you are investing in, it is important that you, the lender, or broker has due diligence. This ensures that everything related to the property and the loan is legally handled, as well as the property being used as collateral for the loan. This ensures that you receive the payments from the borrower and that you are entitled to the property if the borrower defaults for any reason on the loan.

In a recessionary market or a real estate market experiencing stringent lending guidelines, private mortgages are even more popular options for funding. Individuals who may not qualify for a conventional mortgage — savvy real estate investors looking for a quick and easy way to fund their loan — are seeking private money lenders like you. They are ready and able to pay a premium in exchange for the ability to buy the home or property they want to purchase. The premium they pay is a benefit to you, earning you a higher rate of return than other types of investments.

The risks

The main disadvantage of investing your money in private mortgages is its lack of liquidity. Even though these are short-term loans – only lasting up to a maximum of five years – your money is tied up in the mortgage, and you cannot access the cash until the loan is paid off. Remember, if you invest in a private mortgage, you are the lender, so you have given the money to the borrower in order to purchase a property. Your money is gone and the only way you get your money back is when the borrower makes monthly payments to you until the loan is paid-in-full.

The second major disadvantage of private mortgage investing is the possibility of default and foreclosure. During the time the borrower defaults on the loan and until the foreclosure process is complete, you are not receiving monthly mortgage payments from the borrower. You can recover your investment and even turn a profit when you sell the property, but during the foreclosure process, your money is tied up in the home.

How property values affect your investment

Economies change and so does the real estate market; there may be good and bad times to invest in private mortgages. When traditional lending guidelines tighten, making it difficult for borrowers to obtain traditional financing, borrowers turn to nontraditional financing methods, such as private mortgages. Savvy real estate investors or investors who are in a hurry to buy and finance a property are more willing to pay a slightly higher interest rate in a private mortgage because it is a quicker and easier way to obtain financing than maneuvering the red-tape of traditional mortgage lenders. As is true with any type of investment, there are better times than others to consider investing in private mortgages. In general, though, the benefit of investing in private mortgages is that it is secured by a piece of property so you always have the option of foreclosing on the property in case of default by the borrower. In case of default, foreclosure is the avenue to recoup your initial investment and the return on your investment.

Investing in your retirement account

Chapter 10 of this book discusses ways you can use the equity in your property to fund and invest in a retirement account. You can choose to invest in a retirement account through private mortgages. Whether you can put your retirement money in a private mortgage investment depends on the financial institution where your retirement account is held, which is also known as the custodian of the account.

If your retirement account is a self-directed account, then you can choose to use some of the funds to invest in private mortgages. When you invest in an account held by a custodian, they have certain fund families you can choose from to invest your money in. When you have a self-directed account, you are not typically limited to the fund families offered by the custodian, so you can direct the investment vehicles to put your money into. If the custodian does not permit this type of investment, you can transfer the investment amount into a self-directed account that allows you to invest in private mortgages. When investing in private mortgages through your retirement account, you still have the option of establishing your own mortgage note or working with a broker to establish the note on your behalf.

The return on your investment is earned in your retirement account, so you are not paid directly; instead, it is deposited into your retirement account. This is similar to when you are investing your equity money in funding a private mortgage. When the private mortgage comes due, the principal balance payment is also deposited into your retirement account rather than directly to you.

How a Private Mortgage Investment Provides a Return

Whether you hold the promissory note yourself or you choose to invest through a hard moneylender, there are two ways you can earn a return on your investment. First, you receive monthly – or sometimes quarterly – payments on the amount of money you have invested. These payments include a portion of the principal to pay down the loan and a portion of interest. Typically, the interest rate charged is in the double digits, so these rates are higher than the typical bank or lender rates. The rate of return on private mortgages is typically at a higher rate than the typical stock, bond, or mutual fund – especially during a recession or in a declining market, when private mortgages are in more demand because conventional financing is harder to obtain. By the time the loan is paid off, you have earned anywhere from 12 to 15 percent (and, in some cases, more) on the original amount you invested in the private mortgage(s) instrument. This is the ideal and typical situation for an investor who chooses to invest in private mortgages.

The other way that private mortgage investors earn a return on their investment is in the case of default on the property. Because you are the note holder, the deed to the property becomes yours in the case of default. This means that as the owner of the property, you can do with it what you wish. This may mean renting it out to receive rental income, converting it into a different type of property to increase the return on your investment, or selling the property for more than the original amount you invested to gain a profit from the sale.

If you have established a home equity loan or did a cash-out refinance to tap into the equity you have built in a property, then you have the funds to invest in private mortgages. The way you access the funds is slightly different, though, depending on the type of financing you used. If you have an equity line, then the lender will provide you with checks or a debit/credit card to access the line. If you are investing in private mortgages through a hard moneylender or private mortgage broker, then they will tell you what type of payment they accept (checks, cash, credit cards, or money transfers) to fund your investment. When you use the equity line to invest in private mortgages, then you immediately begin to pay interest on the balance you have used on the line. Depending on how often you receive interest payments from the borrower, you can use this money to cover your monthly equity line payments. Any money that is left above that payment is the return on investment for you to keep as a profit.

If you accessed the equity in your home with a cash-out refinance or equity loan, then you received the loan in a lump sum. If you deposited these funds into a checking or savings account, then you would access these funds accordingly in order to get the amount you want to invest to a hard moneylender or private money broker. Again, you can use the payments coming from the borrower to cover your mortgage payments for paying back your own loan.

If you are working directly with the borrower, the process is a little different. If you own the home that the private note is being held on, then how your equity funds are used may vary according to whether you have an existing mortgage on the property. If the equity line or loan is on the property that you are selling, then it requires that you get permission from the existing lender to hold a private note on the property. If you own the property free and clear of any mortgages or liens, then you can hold a promissory note on the property without consulting anyone else first.

In a case where you own the property free and clear, then you are not using your cash to fund a loan to for the borrower, but the scenario requires a promissory note and agreement to be drawn up between you and the borrower. You agree to sell the property in exchange for the mortgage amount you hold on the property as long as the buyer makes monthly principal and interest payments directly to you.

If you do not own the property that the private mortgage is being used to buy, then you will be funding the mortgage. For example, Susie is selling a home and Bobbi wants to buy it. Bobbi cannot qualify for a conventional mortgage, so she comes to you to see if you will loan her the money to buy Susie's home. Everything is handled the same as when you own the home you are funding the mortgage for — as far as the legal paperwork and setting the terms and conditions of the loan is concerned. The only difference is that when the sale of the home is complete, you write a check to Susie for the purchase price of the home, minus any down payment money Bobbi has given directly to Susie or to you. Susie walks away with the sale price of her home, and you hold the note for the mortgage that Bobbi will pay.

Checklist	
✓	Decide if you want to work directly with the borrower or through a third party, such as a mortgage broker or private moneylender
✓	If directly, research and find local real estate investment clubs and condominium associations where you can find potential borrowers to network with
✓	If through a third party, research and find at least three private money mortgage brokers or hard-money lenders you can work with
✓	Contact each interested individual party or broker/lender to evaluate possible investment opportunities

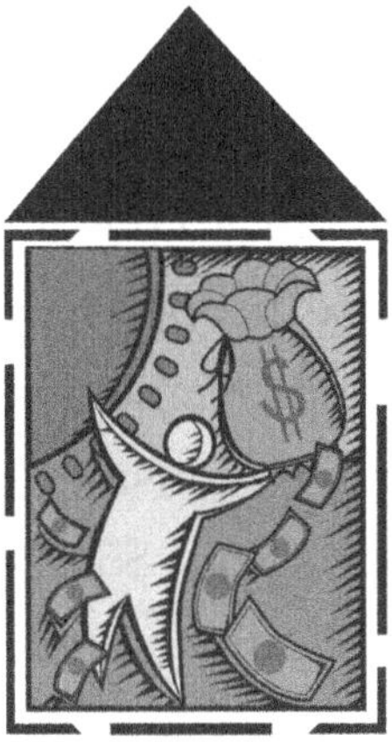

CHAPTER 9

Home Improvements and Renovations

In this chapter you will:

- Learn how to use equity for home improvements and renovations
- Discover how home improvements and renovations can build equity and increase the return on investment
- Understand what types of renovations and improvements increase your return
- Learn the types of properties you can renovate and improve, and how the property type affects your return

One of the most popular uses of home equity funds is putting the money back into your home by making home improvements or renovating the property. In these instances, you are using money from the home to increase the value of that same property. Some consider it more of a reinvestment of the funds rather than an investment. It is important to note a couple of factors about investing your money into a piece of real estate.

First, when you spend money on the supplies and labor involved in renovating or doing home improvements on a property, you do not receive a fixed rate of return on your investment. So, you are not guaranteed or projected to receive 12 percent, 15 percent, or any other percentage, for that matter, because property appraisers do not give a dollar-for-dollar value on improvement because there are many factors that appraisers have to consider to determine property values. This means you may spend $50,000 from your home equity line or loan to renovate your home but only see a 1 or 2 percent return on your investment over a long-term period. The rate of return on your investment is affected by a multitude of factors, detailed later in this chapter.

Second, your rate of return is not a dollar-for-dollar return on your investment. Many homeowners or real estate investors may have the misconception that if they spend $30,000 to renovate the property, then the value increases by $30,000. This, however, is not the case. The value increase of the home or real estate property depends on the type of improvements or renovations rather than the amount of money you spend to make it happen. Compared to other types of investments, you realize or receive the return on your investment differently as well. Investments such as private mortgages or stocks and bonds may pay a monthly or quarterly payment or dividend to you. When you invest your equity funds in home improvements, you do not receive any type of monthly or quarterly payments. In fact, there are only two ways you can receive any return on your initial investment for home improvements.

If you access the additional equity you build in the property after improvements, you can earn a return on your investment because of the increase in the property value, such as if you own a primary residence with a value of $100,000, and the only mortgage you have on the property is a $30,000 home equity line of credit that you established to make renovations to the home. You can spend $30,000 to make the home improvements, which includes ripping out the carpet and adding hardwood floors, refinishing the unfinished basement, and updating the kitchen.

One year later, you decide you want to increase your equity line because you want to buy a duplex as an investment property. You apply for a new equity line in the total amount of $60,000. You estimate the new value of your home is around $120,000, and the appraisal done by the bank shows the house is now that amount. The bank agrees to open an equity line for 85 percent of the value of the home, which gives you $102,000 of equity, but the balance on the existing line has to be paid off first. When the new equity line is established for $102,000, this is inclusive of the $30,000 you originally owed, which leaves an available balance for you to use on the new equity line in the amount of $72,000. With the renovations and the time that has passed, the property value increased. So even after you deduct the payments you have made on the equity line over the past year and the costs involved in setting up the new equity, you have earned a return on your investment.

The second way to receive a return on your investment is to sell the property. If the value of your home or other real estate property has increased because of the renovations, this is a buildup of equity in the property. You can also sell the property for the new market value in order to access the equity that has built up in the property.

CASE STUDY: REHABBING AND RENOVATING

C. Diane Macaulay
Retired College Professor
Ann Arbor, Michigan

C. Diane Macaulay found herself in a situation where she had a low income but good retirement benefits from her past teaching positions at Loma Linda University in southern California and later at the University of Michigan. She decided she wanted to turn the cold storage attic in her home into livable space. When she saw an advertisement from her bank about the possibility of establishing an equity line on her home, she decided to check it out.

After reviewing the equity line terms and conditions the bank provided, Macaulay decided using the equity in her home was the best way to do the renovations to the attic — turning it into a guestroom and office. While she was taking out the equity line with the bank, she also decided to use some of the additional equity in the home to fund the mortgage on purchasing a house in the area that needed to be rehabbed — it needed renovations and to have items fixed in order to make it habitable.

By leveraging the equity she had built up in her home, she has turned her attic into livable space that she uses all the time for herself as well as for guests. The rehab property she bought with the rest of the equity funds she had is now rented out with a long-term lease, so the rental income she receives is also covering some of the cost of repaying the equity loan.

Profiting from Home Improvements and Renovations

Home improvements and renovations are vague terms. There are various subcategories that fall under these two categories. The following pages cover some of the renovations and improvements you can pay for with your home equity funds for the purpose of increasing the value and the amount of equity you have in the property. Your ultimate goal is to earn a return on your investment.

Home improvements — fixing what is broken

One form of home improvement is to fix the various broken items around the home. Whether fixing these items results in an increase in property value depends on what you are fixing. If a major appliance is broken, and you fix the existing appliance or replace it with a new one, it can add value to the property. The same holds true for other necessities, such as plumbing, air conditioning, and heating units and systems. On the other hand, it may only bring the value of the property up to what it should have been originally, because these are necessary items. Remember, the only types of renovations that truly add value to a property include updating kitchens and bathrooms or adding livable square footage to the home. Some states require you to sell a home that includes certain appliances. The home can have both appliances, too, but it is required to have at least one of these major appliances. If you sell a home with a brand new set of kitchen appliances, it can add value to the home and bring you a higher sales price than if you have outdated or old appliances.

Renovating or updating

Another way you can use the money from the equity in your home to increase the value is to renovate or update various areas of the home. If the two major areas of a home that bring you the greatest increase in value are the kitchen and bathrooms — and your home was built in the 1970s with the original kitchen and bathrooms still intact – you can increase the current market value of the home by renovating and updating these rooms. This is also true for plumbing, cooling, and heating systems. Some of the value may depend on the building codes that cover the area where the property is located. For example, if your home were built in the 1920s, and you update the plumbing to meet current building codes and standards, this can and usually does add value to the property.

Energy improvements

Improvements to make homes more energy-efficient and homes that are already energy-efficient can provide you with a return on your investment in a couple of different ways. First, it can save you money on your utility bills. Second, these are selling points for the home when you decide to sell. Third, the federal government is providing tax incentives for real estate property owners that make homes and buildings more energy-efficient. This includes installing energy-saving appliances, windows, solar panels, and more.

For the 2009-2010 tax year, the IRS is allowing homeowners to take a tax credit for up to 30 percent of the cost for energy-efficient home improvements. The credit can be applied for improvements such as adding insulation, energy-efficient windows to keep hot summer air and cold winter air from coming inside, and eco-friendly heating and air conditioning systems. So, on top of increasing the value of your home, you can also use your investment as a tax deduction, which increases the return on your investment even more.

Adding rooms and square feet

The No. 1 way to maximize the increase in property value is to add more square feet to the property, but the key is to add livable square footage; adding bathrooms, enlarging the kitchen, and adding bedrooms are all examples of ways you can add livable square footage to your existing home. This adds the most value because square footage is one of the main factors used in determining property values and sales prices.

For example, assume residential homes where your home is located are selling for $300 a square foot, and your home is currently 1,500 square feet; the current market value of your home is approximately $450,000. Then, you decide to turn your three-bedroom home into a five-bedroom home to accommodate your growing family. Using your home equity line, you build the two additions onto your home. This adds another 288 square feet to your home. This also increases the value of the property from $450,000 to $536,400 (subtract the old value of the home from the new value for an increase of $86,400). It may cost you $20,000 to build the two additional rooms, but you are still netting a return on your money of approximately $66,400 ($86,400 in increased value minus the cost for the renovations of $20,000). You will not be able to cash in on your profit unless you cash out the equity that has been built, or sell the home.

New value of home - Old value of the home = Increased value of the property
$536,400 - $450,000 = $86,400

Increased value of the home - Cost of improvements = Net return on investment
$86,400 - $20,000 = $66,400

Finishing a basement or attic

Refinishing a basement or attic is another way to add value to a home, as it is similar to adding livable square footage to the property. The attic or basement already existed, so it does not change the overall square footage of the home, but it does turn unlivable space into livable space, which is the square footage used to determine the value of the property. So that extra 200 square feet of your now-finished basement can increase the value of your home.

Pools, saunas, and tennis courts

Adding amenities to the property such as a pool, sauna, or tennis court may seem like they add value to the property. In these scenarios, though, value is in the eye of the beholder. It may cost you $20,000 to install and maintain an in-ground pool, but the joy, excitement, and memories it creates for your family does not have a price tag associated with it: Does that mean you can sell your house for more when the time comes?

Not necessarily. What is of value to you may be a deterrent to potential buyers. Some buyers may not have an interest in swimming; more importantly, they may not want to take on the expense of maintaining a pool. So how much of a return is your pool investment going to bring you now? If you have problems selling the property because of the pool, the answer is that it may not even bring you enough in value to cover the cost of installing the pool. On the other hand, some buyers – particularly buyers in warmer climates – find pools to be a premium addition and would be willing to spend more on a home that already has a pool installed. Saunas, tennis courts, racquetball courts, and other specialty amenities may put you in the same position.

Using Equity for Improvements and Renovations

There are a couple of different ways you can use the equity in your property to pay for home improvements and renovations, which is directly connected with the type of financing you establish. If you set up a home equity line of credit, the lender usually provides equity line checks you can use to access the funds. So when you head out to the home improvement store to buy supplies for the renovation, or you pay the contractor or laborer, you can write a check directly to them using the equity line of credit check. When you use the equity line money to pay these expense, you begin to pay interest on the balance you have on the line.

If you have established a home equity loan or did a cash-out refinance to take out the equity you have built in the property, then you have the funds to buy the supplies or hire the labor necessary to make the changes because you received the loan in a lump sum. If you deposited these funds into a checking or savings account, then you would access these funds accordingly for the amount you need to cover the renovation or home improvement expenses.

In a recessionary market or a real estate market experiencing stringent lending guidelines, converting the property use for a higher economic purpose may be one of the best ways to earn a greater return on your investment. *This was covered in Chapter 7, where investing your equity funds in other real estate was discussed.* For the purposes of this chapter, you would be using the equity money to make changes to an existing property to convert it from its current use to a use that has the potential to bring you more money. For example, if you own or purchase a hotel with the intention of making some building modifications to turn it into office suites that you lease out on a monthly basis, you are converting it for a higher economical outcome. Obviously, you want to keep how much you spend for the conversion on budget so that you can recoup the costs from the leasing fees.

Checklist	
✓	Consider the types and cost of renovations or improvements you want to do
✓	Determine the expected rate of return or profit from the renovations or improvements
✓	Figure out how long will it take from the time you spend the money until you see a return on your investment
✓	Check with local zoning and building ordinances to see if the property type complies with all regulations if you are planning on converting the building use
✓	Determine if converting the use of the property affects your rate of return and if it will cost more money to convert because of rezoning and ordinance issues

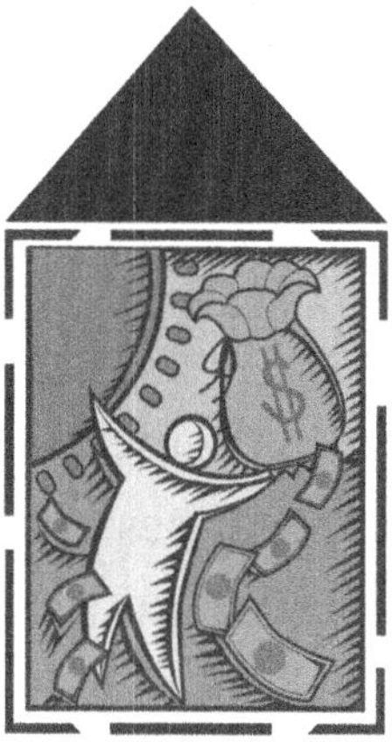

CHAPTER 10

Invest in Your Retirement

In this chapter you will:

- Learn how to build a nest egg for retirement using the equity in your property
- Discover the various retirement account options for you to invest in
- Uncover the advantages and disadvantages to each type of retirement account

Whether you are 20 or 50 years old, planning for your retirement is a looming factor that affects us all; the earlier you start planning for your golden years, the better off you are. There are various ways you can invest your equity to start planning for your future, but investing in a retirement account can be far less confusing than trying to understand the other types of investment accounts you can invest your money in on a personal level. The main types of retirement accounts are:

- Individual retirement arrangement (IRA)
- 401(k)
- Simplified employee pension individual retirement account (SEP-IRA)
- Keogh plans

Do not let the fact that there are only four main retirement accounts to choose from fool you. Within these various types of accounts, you have the option to place your money in various types of investments. There are also some limitations, though. While self-directed retirement accounts allow you to invest directly in real estate, for example, most retirement accounts do not allow investing in real estate. The important thing to remember is to thoroughly research the benefits and limitations of each type of retirement account before making your decision.

Where the real benefit comes in with retirement investing is the tax advantages it can afford you. When you invest and earn a return on your money in a retirement account, you usually do not pay taxes on that amount until you withdraw the money. Think about the implications this can have on building your personal wealth. You can use some or all of your equity to fund and invest in a retirement account, and no matter how much it grows over the 10, 15, 20, or even 30 years you have the account, you do not have to pay any taxes on the money you earn as long as it stays in that account. You are making payments on your equity line to pay back the amount you have borrowed, but you are also deducting all or most of the interest payment you are making on the loan. It becomes a double tax advantage for you.

How Much You Need

The best place to start in the retirement planning process is to figure out how much money you will need to live out your golden years. Knowing how much you think you will need to live the lifestyle you are accustomed to helps you to determine how much money you may need to use from your equity line. It is also important to know how much money you may need to pull from other pools of money, such as employee income or income from your business. You can also consider other sources of income to help fund your retirement lifestyle such as social security, but considering you may have 20 years or more to live after retirement, you want as big of a nest egg as possible to cover your expenses for the rest of your life; the last thing you want to do is outlive your money. Also, with the future of social security unknown, it may not be there for you to access in the future, so it is important not to depend on it as income during your retirement. Even if you are in your 20s or 30s, it is important to start planning and saving for your retirement. If you are already investing for your retirement, it is also important to continue to evaluate your needs. As time goes by, the cost of living increases; so it is important to make sure that the returns on your investments are still projected to cover your living expenses during retirement. Your first step is to calculate how much you need during your retirement.

According to various studies, you typically need approximately 70 to 80 percent of your income prior to retiring to cover your retirement expenses. For example, if you are making $75,000 per year in income now, you will need somewhere in the neighborhood of $52,500 to $60,000 to live out your retirement years in a similar lifestyle as your working years.

This is simply an average, so your needs may differ, depending on your retirement expectations. There are retirees who live on less than what they did before retiring because they do not have expenses such as clothing bills from dry cleaning their professional attire and high gas costs from commuting back and forth to work. Other retirees require more to live on during retirement because with more spare time, they spend more money on traveling, hobbies, or other ways to occupy themselves. It is all a matter of how you foresee your retirement future.

It is important to remember that you are only making projections by using this calculation. It is not an exact science, but it does allow you to estimate how much you may need to save and what rate of return on your retirement investments you need to achieve your goal. It is also important to consider that your retirement account investments may only be one of your income sources. For example, if you are eligible for social security, then determining how much you need to invest in a retirement account is in addition to the monthly benefit you will receive from your social security payment.

While you can crunch some numbers and make some projections for your retirement, you can also take a more professional approach to retirement planning by working with a financial advisor. Advisors also makes projections, but their knowledge and experience in investment management and financial planning may help to guide you into putting your money into retirement investments to help you meet your goals.

Retirement planning worksheet

To give you an idea of how much you need to save and invest to reach your retirement goal, you can use the worksheet below. This is only to be used as guide to estimate how much you may need in retirement because there are some assumptions in the worksheet. First, it assumes you will retire at age 66. It also assumes that the rate of return on your retirement investments is 4 percent above the inflation rate. Note: Not all of the income may be applicable to you.

1.	Estimate the annual income needed for retirement (70 to 80 percent of your current income)	$__________ per year
2.	Annual social security income (Pull from social security statement or **www.ssa.gov**)	$__________ per year
3.	Annual pension payment	$__________ per year
4.	Annual retirement income from personal savings (Subtract lines 2 and 3 from line 1)	$__________ per year
5.	Amount needed to save to retire at 66 (Multiply your answer in line 4 by 15)	$__________
6.	Current value of retirement account	$__________
7.	Projected future value of current savings (Multiply line 6 by the growth multiplier from Appendix A)	$__________
8.	Additional amount needed (Subtract line 7 from line 5)	$__________
9.	Amount needed to save per month to reach goal (Multiply line 8 by the savings factor in Appendix A)	$__________ per month

The amount you need to save or invest on a monthly basis may frighten you. If you are on the right track because you have been saving and investing the right amount to reach your goal, then good for you. More than likely, though, you see a shortfall in what you have been saving and what you should be saving. Now, you have to come up with a plan to get yourself on track to saving the right amount.

There are many ways you can accomplish this, but this section will focus on using your home equity, which typically gives you a decent amount of money to work with to start propelling you toward achieving your retirement needs. This is especially true if you own a home free and clear of any mortgages or liens, where you have a lot of equity built up in the home. You may also be in a situation where you still have a mortgage, but you have a lot of equity built up in it from all of the years of making mortgage payments, the increase in property value since you acquired the property, or from both. Now it is time to ask yourself a very important question: How is a paid-off house going to help you pay your bills when you do not have enough in retirement savings to live on? The same holds true for a home that has a low existing mortgage balance and holds the rest in equity. It is like you are sitting on a pile of money that you could be putting to better use, such as investing now for your retirement later.

Sure: You do not have to send in a monthly mortgage payment, but would it not make more sense to have an income-generating option that not only covers that small mortgage payment, but also food, electricity, and medicine? It is always more beneficial to have money now so that you can invest it later. When you have money now, you can make it grow to fit your needs later — but sometimes, later is too late to start scrambling for money to put it to work.

There are various ways you can tap into the equity of your home. You can take the drastic measure of selling the home to realize your profit and walk away with what hopefully equates to a big, fat check that you can then invest for your retirement. It also typically provides you with enough money to move to a more affordable and possibly smaller home to live out your retirement years. Because retired individuals and couples tend to need less space to live after the children are grown-up and gone, the smart thing to do would be to rent or buy a property that costs you less than the property you just sold. So now you have more of your income left after paying your expenses. *If you do not opt to sell your current home to access the equity you have built up, Chapter 3 explained the ways to pull out the equity in your home that allow you to remain living in your home.* You know that you can use an equity line, loan, or mortgage to tap into the equity that you can use to fund a retirement account or supply additional money to an existing retirement account to ensure you will reach your goal for your golden years.

Types of Plans

Now, let us take a look at all of the retirement account options available to turn your money into a nice, cushiony nest egg for your retirement. Keep in mind as you read through these options that not all of them will allow you to deposit your equity funds for investment; it is important for you to understand the big picture view of creating an investment strategy to help you accomplish your retirement goal. When it comes to retirement investment accounts, there are two main categories: employer-sponsored accounts and self-employed accounts. Each type of account has its own quirks, rules, and investment options associated with it. These are items you need to be aware of because if this type of account alone cannot help you to meet your goals, then it is important you establish the account or mix of accounts that helps you to meet or exceed your goal.

Employer-sponsored plans

When you are an employee of a company or organization, your employer may give you the option to establish and maintain a retirement account through a company with an investment company. It can be financially beneficial to do so because investing in employer-sponsored retirement accounts may be done pre-tax, so the money is taken from your paycheck before the taxes are deducted. It can also be beneficial because some employers match the amount of money you invest in your account, so it is like getting free money for your retirement. It depends on how the employer chooses to establish the plan, but some employers match retirement dollar-for-dollar. This means for every dollar you invest in your retirement account, they will match it. Employers typically cap the amount they will match at either a dollar amount or percentage rate. When you are a company or organization employee, there are typically three types of retirement accounts companies use. These types of accounts include 401(k), 403(b), and 457.

401(k)

A 401(k) is an employer-sponsored retirement account funded from pre-tax dollars taken from each paycheck. Some employers match your contribution dollar for dollar, while others do not match it; some will match a percentage of what you contribute. There are caps set by the IRS as to how much you can contribute to these plans on an annual basis. These caps increase on a scheduled basis in order to try to keep up with the rate of inflation.

403(b) and 457

While 401(k)s are generally used by for-profit organizations, 403(b)s are used for nonprofit organizations; that is the only difference between the two types of plans. Employees of a nonprofit organization can contribute to their 403(b) directly from their paychecks on a pre-tax basis. Another non-profit employee retirement account option is the 457 plan. The main difference between a 457, 401(k), and 403(b) is that a 457 plan does not separate the money you contribute from the finances of the organization. This means if the nonprofit closes its doors, your retirement funds may go with it.

The main difference between a 457 plan and a 403(b) is that with a 457 plan, the organization commingles the organization's funds with the retirement investment funds of its employees. Because the funds are not separate, if the organization folds and the assets of the organization have to be liquidated to pay debts and creditors, your retirement funds can and may be used. The 403(b) plan does not commingle your funds with employee funds, so your funds have more protection than those in a 457 plan. Both the 403(b) and 457 plans are used by nonprofit organizations, while for-profit companies typically use 401(k) accounts.

Self-employed plans

When you own your own business, it becomes your responsibility to establish and maintain a retirement account of your own. This can be a benefit because it allows you to set up and maintain the type of retirement account that best fits your retirement planning. It can also be a disadvantage because you are responsible for establishing and maintaining your retirement account. If you are a procrastinator or do not take the necessary steps to invest in a retirement account, then the opportunity is lost. As a business owner, you are also responsible for establishing retirement plans for employees, but the following will only focus establishing a retirement account for you. When it comes to setting up your own retirement accounts, there are three main options: SEP-IRA, Keogh, and IRA. The IRA is also an option to start and maintain your own retirement account in addition to an employer-sponsored plan or in circumstances when your employer does not provide retirement accounts.

SEP-IRA

Simplified employee pension individual retirement account (SEP-IRA) is a type of retirement plan that does not have a lot of required paperwork to set it up. It allows you to contribute up to 20 percent of your self-employed income in the account each year. There is a maximum amount of investment permitted each year, which changes year to year to accommodate the continually increasing cost of living. You can visit the IRS Web site (**www.irs.gov**) to find the current maximum contribution amount.

Keogh

In past years, Keogh plans allowed for higher annual contribution amounts than SEP-IRA accounts, but now the maximum amounts are fairly equal. The Keogh account does still have benefits associated with it that allow business owners to maximize their own personal retirement account contributions because this type of account allows you to integrate your social security with your Keogh account. This means that the owner of the company (you) is allowed to make a contribution at a higher percentage of your income than other employees of the company. This helps to bridge the gap between what you need and what your social security benefits pay, as social security is capped if you earn a certain amount in income each year.

Individual retirement arrangement

Setting up an IRA account is your final choice for retirement planning if you are self-employed. There is a cap on the amount you can contribute each year, and the figure changes based on the tax year and your age at the time the contribution is being made. For the most current amounts allowed by the IRS, visit **www.irs.gov**. For example, in 2008, the contribution limit for anyone younger than 50 was $5,000. For someone who was 50 or older, the maximum contribution amount was $6,000. For individuals who earn less than the contribution amount, the contribution amount maximum is the amount of your income, which is a regulation that is set by the IRS. Because some business owners do not officially pay themselves a salary, it is important to note that you can only contribute up to the amount of salary or income you show on your tax returns in the form of a retirement account contribution. So if you pay yourself a salary from your business of $1,000 per year, then you can contribute a maximum of $1,000 per year.

Whether the contribution you make to your IRA is tax-deductible depends on several factors, but if you cannot deduct your IRA contribution, then you may want to consider opening a Roth IRA account. For example, a traditional IRA contribution amount cannot be deducted if you or your spouse was covered by an employer-sponsored retirement; you may not be eligible to deduct the amount of the contributions made. Other factors that may prohibit tax deductions for IRA contributions include the amount of your income, your tax filing status (single or joint), and your social security benefits.

If you (or your spouse) are covered by an employer retirement plan, this table helps you to determine if the amount of your deduction for IRA contributions is affected:

IF your filing status is ...	**AND** your modified AGI is ...	**THEN** you can take ...
single or **head of household**	$53,000 or less	a full deduction
	more than $53,000 but less than $63,000	a partial deduction
	$63,000 or more	no deduction
married filing jointly or **qualifying widow(er)**	$85,000 or less	a full deduction
	more than $85,000 but less than $105,000	a partial deduction
	$105,000 or more	no deduction.
married filing separately	less than $10,000	a partial deduction
	$10,000 or more	no deduction

(Courtesy of the IRS: **www.irs.gov/publications/p590/ch01.html#en_US_publink10006114**)

If you are not covered by an employer retirement plan, this table helps you determine if the amount of your deduction is affected:

IF your filing status is ...	**AND** your modified AGI is ...	**THEN** you can take ...
single, head of household, or **qualifying widow(er)**	any amount	a full deduction
married filing jointly or **separately** with a spouse who is not covered by a plan at work	any amount	a full deduction
married filing jointly with a spouse who is covered by a plan at work	$159,000 or less	a full deduction
	more than $159,000 but less than $169,000	a partial deduction
	$169,000 or more	no deduction

married filing separately with a spouse who is covered by a plan at work	less than $10,000	a partial deduction
	$10,000 or more	no deduction

(Courtesy of the IRS: **www.irs.gov/publications/p590/ch01.html#en_US_publink10006114**)

According to the IRS, contributions made to a Roth IRA account are never tax-deductible, which is different from a traditional IRA. A Roth IRA permits you to contribute after-tax money to invest as part of your retirement planning process. Not only that, but the money in a Roth IRA account grows tax-free, too. While you cannot deduct the contribution you make to a Roth IRA, it does not matter because you are contributing from a source of money after taxes have already been deducted.

When it comes time to take distributions from a Roth IRA account, the withdrawal amounts are also made tax-free as long as the distributions are qualified distributions. Qualified distributions are those taken at least five years after the first tax year that a contribution was made into the Roth IRA account. For example, if you made your first-year contribution into your Roth IRA in 2005, then a distribution would not be considered to be qualified until after 2010. The timeframe between the first contribution and the first distribution is not the only requirement for the distribution to be considered qualified and therefore tax-free. The distribution must also be made on or after you are 59 ½ years old; made because of a disability; made to a beneficiary upon your death; or taken to use for a first-time home purchase. Otherwise, early distributions from a Roth IRA are charged a 10 percent penalty fee based on the amount of the distribution you take. So as long as you abide by all of the rules, you can establish, grow, and take distributions from a Roth IRA without having to pay Uncle Sam one dime.

Allocating Money in Your Retirement Account

When you invest in retirement accounts that are sponsored by your employer, you may be limited to the types of investments you can choose from based on the investment firm that manages your retirement account. Obviously, this also has an effect on the rate of return you can earn on your investment. It is important to understand how your funds are or can be allocated because if you do not allocate the funds in the right manner, then you may not reach your retirement goal.

The first type of investments you should avoid in your retirement account is the savings account or money market account options. Essentially, a money market account is the same as a savings account, except the rate of return is typically higher than a regular savings account. Although these types of accounts are seen as safe ways to invest your money because your cash remains liquid rather than invested in stocks, bonds, or other types of investment, savings and money market accounts also offer extremely low rates of return on your investment. This means that investing in these types of accounts can take a lot longer to reach your goal than investing in accounts that pay a higher rate of return.

For example, you make $1,000 per week and plan to use 10 percent of your income to invest in a 401(k) plan or traditional savings account, but you are trying to determine which investment vehicle is most beneficial. Assuming that your federal tax bracket is 28 percent and the 401(k) contribution is exempt from federal taxes, the $100 contribution (10 percent of $1,000 of your weekly gross pay) will lower your net pay by $67 – *not* the full contribution amount of $100. The contribution will not lower your next pay by the full contribution amount because the 401(k) contribution is deducted from your taxable gross amount, while the remaining money is taxed. This means that you are really giving up $67 of your paycheck, but you are saving the full $100 in your retirement account because of the after-tax calculation. Using a regular savings account, however, you would be giving up the full $100 in net pay because regular savings accounts do not have the same tax-exempt feature as the 401(k).

For example, using a simple savings calculator (like the one offered at **www.saveorspend.com/calculator**), you can quickly calculate how much your money would grow by putting $100 per month into a savings account. Assuming that the interest paid on a savings account is 2 percent compounded monthly, then by saving $100 per month, after a 10-year period, your money would grow to $13,271.97.

On the other hand, if you were to invest $100 in a 401(k) account, you can use a 401(k) calculator (such as the one at **www.familycredit.org/future-planning-calculators/retirement-planner**) to figure out your future earnings. If you are putting away $100 per week and assuming an annual rate of return of 9 percent, then after a 10-year period, your money would have grown to $82,803.

Another major advantage of the rate of return you can earn on a 401(k) over a savings account is that employers tend to match contributions made to a 401(k) but do not offer the same matching option for a savings account. Even if the employer only matches your 401(k) contributions by 3 percent, it is still more advantageous to invest in a 401(k) plan over a savings account. In this scenario, where the employer matches your contributions by 10 percent – and assuming the same numbers as those used above in the original 401(k) example – your 401(k) account would then grow to $91,083 instead of $82,801.

Another common investment option in employer-sponsored retirement accounts are bond mutual funds. These types of mutual funds allow you to invest in various types of bonds —typically high-quality bonds. *You will learn more about what bonds are and how they work in Chapter 15.* Bond investments usually pay a higher rate of return than money markets or savings accounts but also have a higher risk associated with investing in it. Typically, you earn less of a return on your investment in a bond mutual fund than you would earn in a properly diversified 401(k) or IRA. You can invest in bonds in your 401(k) and IRA accounts, too. Depending on how you invest your retirement funds, you may earn the same rate as a bond, but generally you earn more in a properly diversified 401(k) or IRA than you do when you invest solely in bonds.

Whether you should invest your money in a bond mutual fund depends on how much time you have left until you retire. The closer you get to your retirement age, the more attractive bond mutual funds are because it is a safer investment than other options. As you near retirement age, you want to preserve the money you have already saved, and you have less time to recoup from significant losses in your account. This is why investing in safer options, such as bond mutual funds, helps you achieve this goal. Young, aggressive investors who have decades left before retiring will not find bond mutual funds the best use of their money because the rate of return is lower than other investment options; at this point in life, they are more interested in growing their money and taking higher risks because they have time to gain back any money lost before retiring.

Employer-sponsored retirement account investments also include balanced mutual funds. This type of mutual fund allows you to invest your money into a mixture of stocks and bonds. Although stocks are deemed riskier investments, bonds are seen as safer investments; thus, by combining the two, you are also balancing the volatility of the return on your investment. Investing in balanced mutual funds is one of the most popular ways for employees to invest the funds that they and their employers contribute to their individual retirement investment account.

You always have the option to invest in stock mutual funds, which combine a variety of stocks. From a long-term standpoint, this investment strategy has the potential to bring you the greatest return on your investment. This type of investment is riskier than the other types of mutual funds mentioned, but less risky than investing in individual stocks. Investing in stock mutual funds is slightly riskier than bond mutual funds because stocks tend to be more volatile than other investments — especially in a rapidly changing stock market and suffering economy. Because a stock mutual fund consists of various types of stocks, it is less risky than investing in individual stocks because the diversification of stocks in the mutual fund helps to balance each other out. So if one stock in the stock mutual fund is in an industry that may be suffering (such as the automotive industry), then a stock in an industry that is booming (such as an international or global company stock), then the downturn in one stock does not cause the total amount of your portfolio to lose money because it is offset by the well-performing stock. While this strategy may not increase the total value of your portfolio, it definitely helps to preserve your total investment amount, which over time helps your investments to continue to grow.

The problem with relying solely on an employer-sponsored retirement account is that you still may not be able to earn enough of a return to reach your nest-egg goal. Because the money invested in an employer-sponsored account is deducted from your paycheck (usually on a pre-tax basis), you do not have the option of contributing money from other sources, such as the equity funds from your home, in an effort to accomplish the retirement goal you have set.

This is where allocating money in self-directed accounts or plans you design comes in handy. You always have the option to open an investment account where you invest additional funds into stocks, bonds, mutual funds, and other types of investments in an individual investment account outside of an account that is designated as a retirement account. *Investing in an investment account like this is discussed in Chapter 15.* Just because the investment account is not one of the accounts mentioned here does not mean that it cannot count toward earning money to use to live out your retirement years.

How your equity plays a role in retirement planning

There are two main ways that the equity you pull out of your home or business may play a role in retirement planning. One way plays more of a direct role, while the other option plays more of an indirect role. If you use your equity line or business equity to fund business activities, this can increase the income of the business. The more money your business makes, the more money you make — and, in turn, the more money you can contribute to retirement planning.

This is a direct approach to pulling equity out of your home because you have to take the step of using your equity to fund sales activities, marketing activities, buying new machinery, and paying the costs of operating the business on a daily basis. On the other hand, it is an indirect approach in that using the equity to pay for business costs is not a situation like investing in private mortgages, where you know what your rate of return is going to be. Investing money in your business could bring a high rate of return — more than the average 14 percent that a private mortgage investment tends to bring — or could bring you a zero or negative rate of return, which would mean that you are only breaking even on your investment or losing money on your investment.

For example, if you use your equity line to expand your business's building to accommodate for a new product line, a couple of things can happen: First, you are usually able to deduct the interest portion of the payments you make to repay the equity line balance; second, adding a new product line should increase the income and the profits of the business. Now that you can pay yourself a higher salary or claim a higher income, you can contribute more money to your retirement account as long as it is within the limits established for the type of retirement account you have.

The types of accounts covered in the last chapter of this book may allow you to directly invest your home equity money into the types of investment vehicles you choose. Some investment accounts prohibit you from directly depositing equity from a home or business into an investment account. However, it is not prohibited to deposit equity funds into a regular checking or savings account, then use the money from your savings or checking account to fund an investment account. So it is possible to indirectly invest equity funds into an investment account to use as part of your retirement savings plan, even if the label of the account does not fall into one of the categories mentioned in this chapter.

Checklist	
✓	Project how much money you will need to live out your retirement years
✓	Consider the types of retirement account options available to you
✓	Decide how you want to invest the money you put into your retirement account

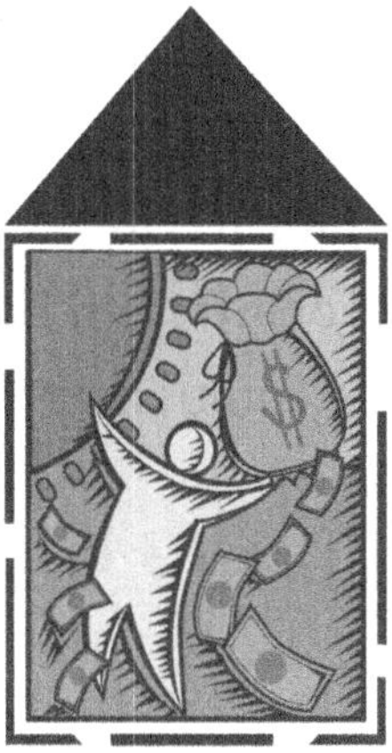

CHAPTER 11

Invest in Your Child's Future

In this chapter you will:

- Determine how much money you need to pay for your child's college education
- Figure out how much you already have
- Decide how to invest your equity money to make up for the shortfall

Saving for your child's (or children's) college education can be as anxiety-producing as making sure you have enough money to make it through retirement. The rising cost of living does not skip over the costs of a college education. Depending on how many years you have until you send your child off to college, a more prestigious Ivy League school could cost you somewhere in the neighborhood of $1 million over four years if you factor in the future value of money. Some of us may never see $1 million in our lifetime, so how can you save that amount of money?

Fortunately, there are several avenues you and your child can use to pay for college expenses. Financial aid, grants, and scholarships are a few of these options. These are not areas you should absolutely depend on, however, so it is important to do your own savings plan to make sure you have the money when the time comes. This may be precisely when using the equity in your home to fund a college education comes into play.

Estimating College Expenses

The costs of a college education consist of more than just the tuition itself. You also have to factor in books, supplies, room and board, and transportation. Then there is the problem that college tuition fees range from $9,000 per year to as much as $50,000 per year, depending on the college or university. According to FinAid (**www.finaid.org**), the average increase for college tuition on an annual basis is 8 percent. Furthermore, if you consider the fact that in that in-state tuition and out-of-state tuition are significantly different, you may have to factor in even more money if your child plans on attending an out-of-state school. As of 2008, the average tuition cost for a four-year private college is $138,000, and a public college is approximately $70,000. This gives you a starting point for how much you will need to save to pay for all four years of college. If you or your children have more expensive tastes in schools, you may want to add another 20 to 30 percent to your estimated costs. Below, you will find a worksheet you can use to help you estimate how much money you need to save in order to cover college tuition costs and living expenses.

1.	Estimated cost of four-year college education	$________
2.	The percentage of the costs you will pay	
3.	Total amount in today's dollars (Multiply line 1 by line 2)	$________
4.	Number of months until your child goes to college	
5.	Amount you need to save per month (Divide line 3 by line 4)	$________

Now that you have a number to work with, it is time to figure out how you are going to turn the money you have today into the money you need tomorrow.

Educational Fund Investment Options

After you have accessed the equity in your home or business using one of the financing methods you learned about in Chapter 3 (home equity line of credit, home equity loan, or cash-out refinance), it is time to figure out what type of investments you can put the money into to earn enough to equal or exceed the amount listed above.

There are investment options available that are specifically geared toward paying for future college expenses. Some states offer a pre-paid program that allows you not only to save for your child's education, but also to lock into today's rates rather than having to worry about how much college will cost in the future. There are some caveats with these programs, though. One is that the child has to attend a school within the state of the program you are investing. If they do not attend one of the in-state schools, you do get your money back — so it is not a total loss — but it is too limiting and is not a way to grow your money.

Financial experts highly recommend no-load mutual funds as a good investment vehicle to invest your money in now to pay for a child's college education later. A no-load mutual fund is one where the mutual find company does not charge an extra fee for the purchase or sale of the mutual fund. When a mutual fund is a load fund, there is an extra fee charged when you buy or sell the fund, which is used by the mutual fund company to cover its costs for matters such as marketing, promotion, distribution and commissions. You can choose whether you wish to invest inside or outside of tax-sheltered accounts. The key to maximizing the return on the no-load mutual fund investments is to gear the investment toward the time period you have until your child needs the money for college. The drawback of no-load funds is that historically they have not outperformed or earned great returns than load funds.

You can also choose to invest on your own in an online account, or you may opt to seek the professional advice of a financial advisor or money manager. If you feel comfortable with researching your own investment options and managing your own investment accounts, there are a multitude of investment firms that allow you to manage the account yourself – online or via phone. Others, however, feel more comfortable relying on a financial advisor's experience and expertise in managing money and investments to help them achieve their goal. Like any do-it-yourself project, managing the investments yourself may turn out just the way you planned, or you may end up scrambling to hire a money manager to correct the errors or problems that occurred along the way.

If you have waited too long to grow your money and your child is off to college in the next few years, it is still not too late. Although you should still apply for financial aid, grants, and scholarships, you can also use the home equity line or equity money you have taken out of the property with another type of loan to fund your child's college education. Need to make a tuition payment? Write a check from your equity line. Dorm payment due? Equity line check. You also may have a big enough equity line to fund all four years of college, deduct the interest portion of the payments from your taxes, and sleep in peace at night because you have the money to cover your child's college education.

If using no-load mutual funds or tapping the equity line to pay for college directly are not right methods for your personal financial situation, you can always go the route of investing in your own stock, bond, and mutual fund portfolio. *Learn more about these methods in Chapter 14.* For example, if a no-load fund charges too high of a fee when you sell it in order to turn it into to cash to pay for college expenses, then this type of investment may not be the best option for paying college costs. At the time you are ready to send your child to college, you may not have enough equity in your home to cover the college expenses. The interest rate on the equity line may also be higher than a standard student loan, which again would make using the equity loan or line on your home less advantageous than taking out a student loan. Other parents may fund their child's college education by investing their equity funds into one of the investment options already covered in this book, such as real estate, then using the return on their investment to cover the child's educational expenses.

For example, a transmission shop owner bought a residential property for each of his three children. He rented the homes out for enough money to cover the monthly mortgage payments on each home. As each child approached college age, he sold the home and used the profit from the sale to pay for college expenses. The way you choose to invest your money in order to pay for your child to go to college depends on how much time you have to save, how much you need to save, and your risk comfort level. The types of investment options available to you are varied, so you have to match your needs and wants with what is available to see which options match your goals.

CASE STUDY: HOME EQUITY TURNING INTO EDUCATION

Philip Marcus
Attorney
Columbia, Maryland

CLASSIFIED CASE STUDIES
directly from the experts

Philip Marcus and his daughter both had big dreams for her future. When his daughter decided to attend a technical school to turn her dreams into a reality, Marcus found himself in a situation where he needed to come up with the money to pay for her tuition. He needed cash, and he needed it quickly to pay off the high-interest-rate student loans that they originally used to fund her education with a lower-interest rate option.

Most of Marcus's cash was tied up in IRAs, and pulling funds from a retirement account would mean he would pay taxes on the amount he used — potentially 30 or 40 percent of the proceeds. Initially, he borrowed from the usual student loan programs, but in terms of interest rates, he felt it was too high and thought there must be a better way.

That is when Marcus thought about a pre-existing home equity line of credit, HELOC, which he had established when he had refinanced his home several years previously. At the time he established the equity line, he never expected to use it; he only established it in case of an emergency. Marcus eagerly watched as the Federal Reserve lowered interest rates, trying to stave off the recession that began around 2007. The interest rate on Philip's HELOC dropped below 4 percent, which was half of the student loan rate he was initially paying to cover his daughter's tuition. Then, Marcus decided to take advantage of the drop in interest rates and wrote a check from the HELOC account to pay off the student loan.

Marcus paid a lower interest rate on the HELOC, and the monthly payment was lower than the student loan payment. Because he paid almost twice the amount of the minimum payment due and only used a small portion of his available equity line, he expected to pay less interest and money in the long run. Plus, his daughter walked away with a career for life.

Checklist	
✓	Determine how much money you need to pay for your child's college education
✓	Determine how much money you already have saved to cover college expenses
✓	Decide which investment options allow you to use the equity in your home money to make up for the shortfall between what you need and what you have saved

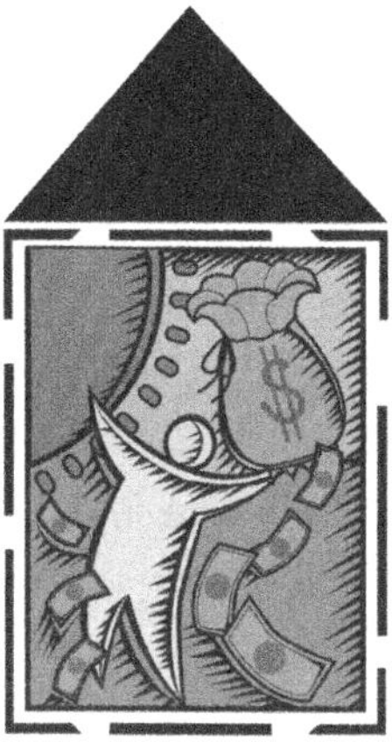

CHAPTER 12

Paying Off Bad Debt

In this chapter you will:

- Learn how to use your equity to pay down, pay off, or consolidate debt
- Discover how it may benefit you to use your equity to get rid of certain types of debt
- Uncover which debts may need to be paid off

There is good debt, and then there is bad debt. Good debt covers the type of debt that is tax-deductible, such as the interest paid on a mortgage or student loans. Good debt also has a lower interest rate than bad debt. Bad debt is also referred to as consumer debt and covers the types of debt that typically are not tax-deductible and have a high rate of interest associated with it, such as credit cards, auto loans, and furniture loans.

CASE STUDY: PAYING OFF OUTSTANDING LOANS

Danny Kofke
Special Education Teacher
Author of "How To Survive (and Perhaps Thrive) On A Teacher's Salary"
www.dannykofke.blogspot.com

Special education teacher and author Danny Kofke and his wife found themselves almost debt-free. They had a mortgage on their two-bedroom house, student loans in the amount of about $5,000, and a car loan on which they owed approximately $10,000.

With a growing family, they decided they wanted to put an addition on their Florida home to turn the two-bedroom home into a three-bedroom home. They decided the best route for them to take was to pull the equity out of their home to pay for the cost of adding the bedrooms. In addition, they decided to take out an additional $15,000 to pay off the outstanding car and student loans.

While they paid off the outstanding loans, they delayed putting the addition onto the home. Instead, they relocated from Florida to Georgia. The Kofkes used the equity line on their Florida home for the down payment on their Georgia home. When they sold their Florida home, they received enough in the sale to pay off the existing mortgage, which left them debt-free except for the mortgage on the Georgia home.

With only a mortgage debt, Kofke's wife is a stay-at-home mom, and they are able to live comfortably on his teaching salary.

Debt Consolidation

Another beneficial way to use your equity line, loan, or mortgage is to pay down or completely pay off your debt — especially your bad debt. Typically, an equity line, loan, or mortgage offers a lower rate of interest, so using it to consolidate your debt turns bad debt into good debt, and you will pay less interest in the long run than you would trying to pay each debt separately. Second, it turns debts that are usually not tax-deductible into tax-deductible ones.

It is important not to over-borrow on your home, no matter what you plan on doing with the money you pull from the equity in the property. When consolidating debt, it is also important to make sure that by consolidating the debt, you are paying a lower interest rate on the new debt. Finally, it is important to consider the after-tax benefits as well. The following example illustrates how using an equity line to consolidate debt can be beneficial:

Zoe's list of debt

Student loans	$12,000 balance at a rate of 4.875%
Credit card #1	$10,000 balance at a rate of 17%
Credit card #2	$5,500 balance at a rate of 22%
Furniture loan	$3,000 balance at a rate of 13%
Auto loan	+ $14,000 balance at a rate of 8%
Total debt	$44,500

Right now, Zoe is in debt $44,500. If you take the average of the interest rates she is currently paying, you will find that it is about 12.975 percent. Because most equity lines have not seen an interest rate in the 12 percent range since the 1980s, it is safe to say Zoe would be better off consolidating her debt because she will be paying less interest. This is not even taking into consideration the money she will save each month by reducing her payments or the after-tax cost if she uses an equity loan to consolidate her debt, because the interest paid on an equity line is generally tax-deductible.

It is easy to use the equity in your home to consolidate your debt. Once you have established the financing to tap into the equity, you simply contact the creditor you owe money to, determine the payoff balance, and write a check or make a bill payment from your equity funds to pay off the debt. It is similar to making a credit card balance transfer. Once you pay the creditor off with your equity line, you now make one payment to your mortgage lender rather than the multiple payments you are currently making to all of the different creditors. So rather than owing each individual creditor a payment each month, you only have to make one payment to the company that holds your equity loan or line.

It is not always necessary to consolidate all your debt, either. For example, in Zoe's situation, she is paying a very low interest rate on her student loan, and this type of debt is typically tax-deductible. If the student loan interest rate is lower than the typical mortgage or equity line rate, then it may be beneficial to consolidate the other debt and leave the student loan as it is.

If you remove the student loan from Zoe's consolidation efforts, you will see it is still beneficial to consolidate with the equity money. Generally speaking, student loans usually have low interest rates and are tax-deductible debts. For this reason, Zoe may choose to keep her student loan as is but consolidate the rest of her debt using her equity line.

Make a list of your debt

Now it is your turn to make a list of your debt to analyze whether consolidating your bad debt with an equity line is the way to go for your personal financial situation. Use a spreadsheet on your computer, or a piece of paper and pen, to create a table that lists out all of your debt, the interest rate you are paying, and the current monthly payment. Compare these totals to what you could be paying if you tap into the equity you have built up in your home, as illustrated in the Zoe example. This helps you to determine whether debt consolidation with the equity line is the best choice.

You can use the following table to help you set up your own expense chart. The equity line balance and interest rate column allow you to compare what you are paying now on your debt with what you would be paying if you pay off the existing debt with the equity line.

Expense Balance	Interest Rate	Monthly Payment	Equity Line Balance	Equity Line Interest Rate

Once you have your list of debts on paper, it is easy to see which expenses have high interest rates and which are low. To truly simplify the debt-consolidation process, most consumers choose to pay off all their outstanding debt with their equity line so that they only have one payment to make each month. This not only helps you to pay less interest in the long-run, but also makes paying your bills each month faster and easier. This is assuming that you have enough of an equity line to cover consolidating all your outstanding debt.

If you are in a situation where you do not have enough equity to consolidate your outstanding debt, then you have to choose which debts you will consolidate. Your first step in this evaluation is to look at the balances and the interest rates you are being charged; you want to pay off the debts with the highest balances and the highest interest rates first.

The second thing you want to take into consideration is the ability to deduct your debt on your tax returns. Certain debts, such as the interest portion of your student loan payments, are tax-deductible, while other debts, such as credit card interest, are not. Because credit cards typically have higher interest rates and are not tax-deductible like student loans, you will want to focus on consolidating these debts first.

One more thing: When you sell the home, then as long as you sell it for more than the balance you owe on the property, you walk away with all the consolidated debt paid in full. If you sell the home for the same amount as the balance of your mortgage, you will break even. If you sell the home for less than what you owe, however, you will have to pay to cover the difference. Typically, even in this situation, you have paid less in the long run with the interest on the equity line or mortgage than you would have if the debt stayed as bad consumer debt.

For example, in Zoe's situation, most of her debts are "bad" debt: credit cards and an auto loan. One of Zoe's debts is considered "good" debt: her student loan. Not only is her student loan tax-deductible, but it also has a low interest rate. If Zoe only has enough money from the home equity line to consolidate a certain amount of debt, then she should focus on the high interest rate credit cards and auto loan first. The same holds true for your own personal situation. If you have to pick and choose which debts you can consolidate, be sure to focus on setting up a plan that is the most beneficial to you and your finances. There is no one-size-fits-all debt consolidation plan, but putting this information down on paper helps you see exactly what you should focus.

A big mistake that many consumers make when using their equity line to consolidate debt — especially bad debt — is when they use this as an opportunity to go back out into the world and run up their debt again. They pay off credit cards, furniture loans, and auto loans at high interest rates, then turn around and start charging up their credit cards again. This behavior defeats the purpose of consolidating debt, so once you have your debt situation under control, do not sabotage your efforts by putting yourself back into debt again. If it means cutting up your credit cards to keep yourself out of debt, then get out the scissors and cut each card up. Use the debt consolidation as an opportunity to get your finances in order and your life back on track.

The question then becomes: "What do we do with all the extra money we are saving each month with the new consolidated debt payment?" It is a good question, and one that has a couple of different answers. First, you can choose to use some of this "extra" money to pay off an additional principal on the equity line in order to pay off the equity line or mortgage on the home faster. The other option is to invest in an outlet that can help you grow your money. It may be that you invest some money in a stock portfolio, or you save up for a down payment on the purchase of a piece of real estate. Whatever way you choose to spend this money, spend it wisely: Spend it on something that is going to bring you more in return, rather than plunging you further into debt.

CASE STUDY: WHEN CREDIT CARDS GO BAD

Peoples Income Tax, Inc. & The Income Tax School
Charles (Chuck) E. McCabe
Founder, President, and CEO
www.peoplestax.com
www.theincometaxschool.com

Chuck McCabe has been using credit cards and unsecured credit lines (personal and business) to provide seasonal financing for his business for years because he could not qualify for conventional bank business financing. His core business of tax preparation began losing market share due to increased competition from national tax firms, DIY tax preparation programs, and volunteer tax services. In the meantime, he started to develop a tax-preparer education business to combat the seasonal cash flow issue. McCabe watched as the business lost about 40 percent of its clients and incurred significant expenses for developing the educational curriculum, e-learning systems, and e-commerce.

This resulted in closing down offices and cutting business expenses. Then in fall 2008, the credit card companies started reducing or eliminating McCabe's credit lines, increasing interest rates, and changing terms. The credit card companies' actions delivered a further blow to McCabe's business despite the fact that he usually paid early, paid more than the minimum required payment, and never missed a payment. This happened to a lot of good credit borrowers during the economic decline that started in 2007 and carried over into 2009. Once again, he approached a bank for conventional business financing but was turned down.

With no other option to obtain money to replace the credit card and non-bank credit lines, McCabe turned to refinancing his personal home mortgage to do a cash-out refinance to pull additional cash out of the property.

A community bank business loan officer advised him that a cash-out refinance would consolidate the existing first and second mortgage, which would allow the bank to collateralize a business loan with the remaining equity in the home — putting the bank lien in second-lien position.

The longer mortgage term of 15 years reduced McCabe's monthly payments and created a situation where the interest portion of the mortgage payment became a tax-deductible debt. He treats this as a personal loan to the business, so the business pays a higher interest rate for the loan (easily justified due to the risk), which enables him to increase his income without raising his pay and having to pay additional payroll tax.

McCabe used some of the cash-out money to pay off some of the highest interest credit cards, and the remainder was deposited into the company business bank account to pay off-season operating expenses. This enabled the business to get through the off-season months of May, June, and July without borrowing from high-interest rate credit cards. It also puts the business in a position to be considered for a bank business loan to pay off the remaining credit card balances and a seasonal line of credit to meet seasonal cash shortage without borrowing from credit card companies.

The business had a profit during the 2008 fiscal year due to cost-cutting and the increased tax school revenue, and McCabe expects to have a better profit for the 2009 fiscal year.

Checklist	
✓	Determine if and how much bad debt you have
✓	Evaluate your equity to ensure you have enough to pay off the bad debt
✓	Determine how much it will save you in monthly payments and interest to consolidate your bad debt with the equity in your property

LIBERTY
UNITED STATES OF AMERICA
QUARTER DOLLAR
IN GOD WE TRUST
2000

CHAPTER 13

Invest in You and Your Family

In this chapter you will:

- Learn unconventional ways to spend your equity funds
- Discover how investing in insurance can protect you, your family, and your assets

An often-overlooked way of investing your money is to buy insurance policies to protect all of your assets. Most people choose not to deal with establishing insurance policies because they relate it to negative happenings in life: death, disability, health issues, and natural disasters. If you look at it from another point of view, you will soon realize that it is worth spending some of your equity funds now to insure against the negative things that happen in life that could drain our wallets. It is usually less expensive to buy a policy to insure your home from loss than it is to replace it.

While an insurance policy may not bring you a hard return on your investment — it is unlikely to yield a 10, 15, or 20 percent return as you would with a stock or mutual fund investment — it will pay you when a certain event such as a natural disaster, death, or injury triggers the payment. There are also some policy types that accrue interest and pay dividends, which will be covered later in this chapter. For now, focus on three main types of insurance that everyone should have to protect the biggest assets: life, health, and disability.

Types of Insurance

Throughout this book, you have learned the various ways you can invest your money today to enjoy it tomorrow. Insurance is a slightly different type of investment because you are investing your money today in case something happens tomorrow. The recipient of the return on investment depends on the outcome. The policy will help you cover the costs of health care, treatment, and medications if you are diagnosed with an illness. Your family may receive the insurance policy funds if you die. This is especially true if your family depends on your income to live.

Life insurance

Many might avoid reading this chapter because few want to think about their own death, but it is important to consider using the money you are sitting on as equity in your home to protect your family against any future malice that may come your way. Similar to retirement income where social security benefits can be received, life insurance provides additional income to your family.

There are two main types of life insurance: term life and cash value. While there are some exceptions to the rule, it is usually most beneficial to invest in term life insurance. You will hear quite a different story if you contact some local insurance agents because commission levels vary based on the types of the policies they sell you; typically, commission rates are higher on cash-value policies than they are on term life policies. In this book, however, you will find the hard truths about the two types of insurance and why term life is a better investment than cash value for most individuals.

Term insurance is straight life insurance; you establish the amount of the policy and pay monthly premiums based on the amount of the policy. If you die, your beneficiaries are paid the amount of the policy. You do not receive a refund of your premium payments unless you die.

Cash value policies are also referred to as whole life, universal life, and variable life insurance. These types of policies are beneficial because not only are you buying an insurance policy, but these types of policies also have a savings account feature. So every month you pay your premium, the premium covers your life insurance policy, and a portion of your premium goes into a savings account. It sounds too good to be true, right? Your instincts are correct because to receive the savings account feature, you will pay eight to ten times the price you will pay on a term policy. It will cost you less to put some of the money that would be going into the savings account feature into your own savings account and simply buy a term policy. The exception to this rule is usually with individuals who have an extremely high net worth in the millions of dollars range. In these scenarios, it may be more beneficial to consider cash value policies over term life policies because those with worth several million dollars have estate-planning needs that justify purchasing a high cash value life-insurance policy.

You should speak to a financial planning advisor and include insurance planning as part of your overall financial and estate planning. These professionals can help you determine which type of policy best fits your needs and how much life insurance coverage you should buy. There is not a straight calculation that gives you the magic number on how much coverage you should carry, although you will hear some insurance agents say it should be seven times your current annual income. Others say it should be enough money to cover your expenses from now until the time you retire. If you are trying to get an idea of how much coverage may be enough for your family, you can use the life insurance calculator provided by the nonprofit organization Life and Health Insurance Foundation for Education (LIFE) at **www.lifehappens.org/life-insurance/life-calculator**.

Disability insurance

Disability insurance also protects your income in case something happens and you can no longer work or make as much money as you do now. Unlike life insurance, disability insurance covers you while you are out of work but not when you die. But, like life insurance, it is an investment in your future and the future of your family income.

In the case of investing in your future, you should mainly focus on long-term disability insurance, which pays you if you cannot work for an extended period of time (usually more than one year) because of an injury that prohibits you from performing your job duties. Being out of work for a couple weeks or a month (which is considered short-term disability) will have a drastically different effect than if you are out of work for a year or are not able to return to work at all.

Short-term policies may not be worth your investment because savings or other forms of cash equivalents (liquidating stocks, bonds, mutual funds, or other types of liquid investments) can be used to cover expenses for a two-week or two-month period. Also, your employer may offer a short-term policy at no additional cost to you. Long-term disability polices, however, can really pay off because they help you to continue to pay your monthly bills for an extended period of time, so you do not have to deplete your savings or liquidate investments to cover when you can no longer work.

Similar to life insurance, there is not a hard-and-fast rule about how much coverage you should buy in a disability insurance policy. Because it comes down to covering your monthly expenses while you are unable to work, you can use the disability calculator on LIFE's Web site at **www.lifehappens.org/disability-insurance/disability-calculator**. Again, the calculator gives you an estimate, but speaking with a financial advisor helps you to better assess how much coverage you may need because it takes all your financial needs into consideration.

Health insurance

Health insurance also protects you and your current income, but it can have an adverse affect on your future income. If you become ill, treatments, doctor visits, and medications can quickly drain your bank account. If it is an illness, such as cancer, that prohibits you from working for a period of time or returning to work at all, it can make your financial picture look even bleaker. Health insurance differs from disability insurance because health insurance only covers your medical expenses. Disability insurance sends you a check each month, which you can use to pay for living expenses. A health insurance policy is not going to send you a check for living expenses, but rather pay the hospital and doctor for medical services performed. If your employer does not offer health insurance as part of your employee benefits package, or you are self-employed, this is a type of insurance that you do not want to overlook.

While life, disability, and health insurance policies are ways to cover yourself, there are also policies to protect your other assets such as your home, cars, and property against liability. Protecting your other assets can be just as important. If your home is destroyed in a natural disaster, you have a car accident, or someone sues you for an injury he or she incurred on your property, you may find your bank account drained from legal fees, claims, suits, or rebuilding costs if you do not have insurance that protects these assets.

Annuities

An annuity is an insurance investment, but it has characteristics of both an investment and an insurance policy. If you invest your money in an annuity, you are investing your money (paying your premium) during the accumulation phase of the annuity. The money invested in an annuity grows and accumulates interest. Similar to a retirement investment account, if you withdraw money from your annuity before you turn 59 ½, then you pay a penalty on the amount of money you withdraw from the account. What makes an annuity different from a retirement account is there is not a limit on the contribution amount you can make, so many investors use annuities as an additional retirement planning tool. An annuity is a form of insurance because an insurance company holds the annuity account.

So how does an annuity work like insurance? If you as the investor die during the accumulation phase, the beneficiary of your annuity is paid the amount of your contribution into the annuity. If you have paid $1 million into your annuity (remember that there is not a contribution amount limit), then your beneficiary receives $1 million. If you use an annuity as a retirement investment or long-term investment, you can start making withdrawals from the annuity after you turn 59 ½ to avoid paying early withdrawal tax penalties.

Universal Life Indexed Products

Especially after 9/11, many individuals went out in search of safe products and investments. An increased popularity in products such as indexed universal life insurance contracts — also referred to as equity index university life (EIUL), fixed index universal life, or investment-grade insurance contracts — and indexed annuities emerged. It has been reported that many Nobel Laureates in economics, Charles Schwab investment guides, and billionaires such as Warren Buffet have used equity index funds for their investments — in fact, index funds that charge minimal fees are one of the best ways to own common stocks.

Whereas variable life insurance policies and variable annuities put the risk on the policyholder, indexed universal life policies put the risk on the insurance company. Universal life products do not guarantee a big rate of return on your investment; however, these types of policies do guarantee a minimum rate of return on your investment, even when the market return rate is less than the guaranteed amount. In other words, even when the market is down, indexed universal life policies retain its value, so it is a safe investment for maintaining principal value.

As an added bonus, when the market is performing well, owners of indexed universal life policies enjoy the increased value in their policies. Because the risk for this type of investment is on the insurance company, these types of investments do not require registration with the Securities and Exchange Commission (SEC) like stocks and mutual funds do. Technically, indexed universal life policies are not considered investments. The bottom line is that indexed universal life policies are considered fixed insurance products rather than securities.

The returns on these types of policies are connected with one of the major market indices such as Standard & Poor's 500 (S&P 500), Standard & Poor's 400 (S&P 400), Dow Jones Industrials, NASDAQ, or Russell 2000. Which index your indexed universal life policy is associated with can vary by the insurance provider, so you will need to discuss this with the insurance company representative. The connection to the index does not mean the money in your indexed universal life policy is invested in these indices. Indexed universal life policies are invested in fixed vehicles managed by the insurance company, mortgages, and conservative bonds.

Using Equity for Insurance Policies

Once you have the equity line, loan, or mortgage set up to access your equity funds, investing in any type of insurance is as easy as making a payment. For insurance policies that have a monthly premium, you can pay the premium using your equity funds. If you choose to invest in an annuity, you can fund the annuity in lump sums or make periodic payments into the policy. All of this can be done with your equity line checks or by writing a check from the bank or brokerage account where you have deposited your property's equity money.

Checklist	
✓	Determine what you need to cover with insurance protection
✓	Evaluate the types of insurance you need
✓	Determine the amount of coverage you need for each type of insurance

TOCK & BOND

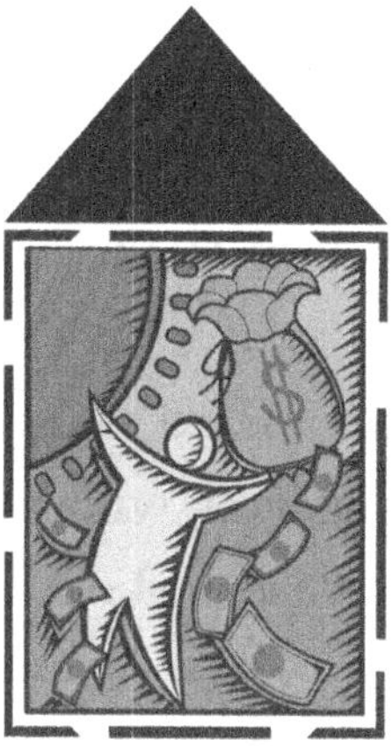

CHAPTER 14

The Other Investment Choices

In this chapter you will:

- Learn how to invest your equity in stocks, bonds, mutual funds, and other types of investments
- Discover the advantages and disadvantages of putting your money into investment portfolios

Whether you are considering allocating your funds into a retirement account or investing your equity funds into a straight brokerage account, it is important to understand what your investment options are. This chapter goes into detail about the investments you can choose when you open a brokerage account. Depending on where you open your account, there may be some limitations on the investment options available to you, but here you will find the information you need to understand each type of investment.

Bonds

When you invest your money in a bond, in essence, you are lending your money to a particular organization or entity. Bonds are set for a specific period of time, which is referred to as the maturity date. The principal amount you invested in the bond is repaid to you by the maturity date. You also earn a fixed rate on your investment with the interest that a bond pays you, which is usually received in two equal payments per each year the bond is outstanding. For example, if you purchase a five-year, 4 percent bond issued by XYZ Company, then you will receive semi-annual interest payments at the rate of 4 percent per year for the next five years. At the end of the five years, you will also receive your original principal investment back.

Characteristics of a bond

Like any type of investments, bonds have different characteristics that you need to be aware of before choosing which ones to invest your money in:

- **Institution issuing the bond**: The first characteristic is what type of organization or entity is issuing the bond. This is the type of institution you are going to be lending your money to. The types of institutions that issue bonds range from municipalities or state governments (municipal bonds), the federal government (treasuries), mortgage lenders (Government National Mortgage Association, which is more commonly known as GNMA or Ginnie Mae), or corporate bonds, where the borrower is a private or public corporation.

- **Quality**: The quality of the bond refers to the credit of the entity issuing the bond. This ultimately determines the likelihood that you will receive your principal investment back upon maturity of the bond. So the better a company's credit rating, the better its bond.

- **Maturity**: There are long-term and short-term bonds, so you also need to consider how long you want your principal investment to be tied up in the bond. Maturity dates for bonds range from as little as three years up to as much as 30 years. Generally, the longer the maturity date, the higher the interest rate and vice versa.

Bond ratings

Major credit-rating agencies make it a bit easier for you to determine the quality of a bond. There are currently three credit agencies that rate bonds: Moody's Investor Service, Standard & Poor's, and Fitch Ratings. There is a safety system that rates bonds, where AAA or AA bonds are the safest, A or BBB bonds are considered slightly less safe, and BB or junk bonds are of lower quality. A bond rating is similar to your credit score. If you have a good credit history where you manage your credit well and make your payments on time, then you will have a high credit score. If your payments are always late and sometimes you do not make your payments at all, then you are going to have a low credit score. If a bond issuer has a good credit history, then its bonds will have a higher bond rating than issuers that do not have a good credit history. While each of these bond-rating agencies provides a credit rating to each bond, each agency also makes information about the bond (and the issuer) available to possible investors to research and draws their own conclusions about the company issuing the bond. In general, though, bonds are considered to be a safer investment option than stocks or mutual fund for two reasons. First, bond interest is paid to bond holders before the dividends are paid to stockholders. Second, the chance of not being paid on a bond is slim, unless the company files for bankruptcy, while not being paid on a stock you invest in occurs at a much higher rate.

Advantages and disadvantages

One of the benefits of investing in a bond is that the value of the bond tends to move with the change in interest rates. This can be advantageous in a falling interest rate environment. For example, if you buy a bond today that yields 6 percent, and interest rates in comparable newly issued bonds are being sold at a yield of 4 percent, then the value of your bond increases. Because your bond yields a higher return than what is currently selling in the market, there would be more interest in buying your bond than one that yields a lower amount. This same concept can be a disadvantage in the event that interest rates are rising. If you hold bonds that yield the same 6 percent rate, and comparable newly issued bonds are yielding 8 percent, then your bond is less valuable.

Some bonds can also have variable interest rates rather than fixed interest rates. This can be beneficial to you if you buy a bond with a low yield and interest rates are expected to increase. For example, one type of variable rate bond allows you to invest in bonds to fund adjustable-rate mortgages (ARMs); when you invest in this type of bond, you are indirectly lending money to the mortgage borrower.

If the bond you buy is a callable bond, then the bond issuer can call the bonds before the maturity date, which means that the bond issuer will pay you back your principal before the maturity date. As compensation for calling the bond early, the issuer typically pays you a premium over the current value of the bond.

Though you cannot necessarily pick the best time in the market to invest in bonds or any other type of investment vehicle, you can watch what interest rates are doing by viewing the printed interest rates in *The Wall Street Journal* or your local newspaper — usually in the money or financial section. News stories in print publications and on TV also cover what is happening with the stock market and current interest rates. This information acts as an indicator on what interest rates are expected to do and can help you to determine when you may want to buy bonds. The Federal Reserve makes announcements periodically on the interest rate environment and what actions it may take for raising or lowering interest rates. Because this is one of the most important government agencies when it comes to interest rates, its actions typically set the tone for how the stock market, bonds, and other rate-based products will work.

Stocks

You may be very familiar with the term "stock" but might have only a small amount of knowledge when it comes to investing. Stocks are issued by public companies, and when you buy stock in a company, you are buying ownership in that company. As the company grows, expands, and earns higher profits, the price of the company's stock also increases. If you sell a stock at a higher price than what you paid to buy it, then you earn a return on your investment. In good economic times, stocks can earn double-digit returns, but a bad economic situation can cause the opposite effect.

The major difference between investing in a company stock and investing in a company bond is that with a stock, you have the potential of losing your initial investment. A stock means that you own a share of the company, but the company is not required to pay you dividends or interest, or even guarantee you a return of any kind. A bond, on the other hand, is an agreement that the company will pay back your initial investment during the bond period as well as make interest payments to you while the bond is outstanding. You could think of a bond like a loan, where you are the lender and the company or institution issuing the bond is the borrower, so not only does the issuer have to pay you back the principal amount they took as a loan, but they also have to pay you interest on the money they have borrowed from you.

The benefit of investing in a stock over a bond is that the stock has the potential to earn you a greater return than a bond. In reality, it all comes down to the risk you are willing to take. If you are conservative and want to preserve your initial investment, then a bond may be the better investment option for you. On the other hand, if you are more of a risk taker and an aggressive investor, then investing in a stock can pay off for you in the long run. If you decide to invest your money by buying stocks, you can choose to manage the account on your own or work with a financial advisor or money manager. If you decide to go it alone, then you will have to do your own research and conduct your own buying and selling of your stocks or bonds. If you work with a money manager or financial advisor, these professionals have knowledge and experience in financial matters that may help you choose stocks and bonds that can help you to better achieve your investment goals than if you try to do it yourself, without their experience and knowledge to back you up.

Mutual Funds

When you invest your equity in a mutual fund, you are investing your money in a group of various stocks. A mutual fund manager chooses the individual stocks to be grouped together to create the mutual fund. When you invest your money in a mutual fund, you are ultimately investing in the money manager's ability to make the right buying and selling decisions. Compared to buying individual stocks, however, mutual funds are a safer investment because of the diversification of the stocks that make up the mutual fund.

You can think of mutual funds as an investment option that has some built-in diversification that helps to balance your portfolio of investments. Because mutual funds are made up of a bundle of different stocks, when one stock in the mutual fund is down, it may be offset by another one of the stocks that is climbing to the top. Some exceptions to this are when a mutual fund focuses on a particular industry or sector in the market. For example, if a technology mutual fund is made up of a variety of technology stocks, then if the technology market is suffering, the value of the entire mutual fund may be down. On a good note, if the technology sector is booming, chances are good that your mutual fund is increasing in value.

Some mutual fund companies allow you to invest your money directly with them. The downside of this is that you are limited to investing your money in the mutual funds offered by this particular company. This is also referred to as the "family of funds" — funds offered by a certain mutual fund company. You also have the option of investing in mutual funds on your own through an online brokerage account or through a financial advisor or money manager. The benefit to investing on your own or through a money manager is that it usually opens the door to a variety of mutual fund options rather than mutual funds offered by one company.

Equity funds

An equity fund is a type of mutual fund where the primary investments are stocks. Though other types of mutual funds may invest in a combination of stocks and bonds, equity funds offer a grouping of stocks. An equity fund is more volatile than investing in a regular mutual fund because stocks are more of a volatile investment — with equity funds, there is always the possibility that you will lose everything. However, that can go the other direction, and you could earn a very high return on investment. By combining individual stocks into a group, however, equity fund investments are less volatile and less risky than investing in straight stocks.

Real estate investment trust (REIT)

A real estate investment trust is a type of investment that also works similarly to a mutual fund. Instead of a combination of stocks and bonds that typical mutual funds invest in, a REIT is made up specifically of real estate investments. REITs invest in various types of commercial real estate such as shopping centers and apartment complexes. REITs are traded on the major stock exchanges and offer investors an opportunity to invest in real estate without physically owning, operating, and maintaining a piece of property.

The major advantage in investing in REITs is that it allows you to own real estate without the hassle of being a landlord. Real estate investment management companies manage REITs and are involved in purchasing and managing investment properties such as warehouses, office building, apartment buildings, and other commercial real estate properties. In order to invest in REITs, you can purchase one on the major stock exchanges, as you would a stock or mutual fund. You also have the option of buying a real estate mutual fund that invests in a variety of REITs.

Mutual funds that invest in real estate are considered specialty funds because they focus investments on a specific industry – real estate. Investing a portion of your portfolio in REITs or a real estate mutual fund can help to diversify your investment portfolio because these types of investments seem to fare better in high inflationary times. As is the case with any type of portfolio, it is not necessarily wise to invest a large portion of your portfolio in REITs.

Index Funds

While mutual funds tend to have fund managers who decide which investments the mutual fund holds, computers primarily manage index fund investments. Index funds consist of a variety of assets chosen to mimic the investments of highly popular index funds such as the Standard & Poor's 500 (S&P 500), which is an index made up of the stocks of the top 500 U.S. companies.

In the long run, over a 10-year or more period, index funds tend to perform better and bring higher rates of returns than almost all the fellow investments a person manages. In fact, index funds consistently outperform approximately three-quarters of all individually managed counterparts.

Index funds use a computer-based software system to predict moves in the market and make decisions on what it should invest in. The computer-based decisions remove any human errors that a team of money managers and analysts could bring to a typical fund. It also comes down to operating costs. Because index funds do not have to pay a high salary to a team of analysts, index funds cost less to operate, which brings a higher rate of return to those who invest in this type of fund.

One of the main advantages of investing in index funds is that it is almost impossible for it to perform worse than the market. When you invest in index funds in your retirement account, there is a bonus advantage: Because there is less trading of the investments in an index fund, the taxable capital gains distributions are lower than other funds. In the end, you end up paying less in taxes with an index fund than with another type of fund.

How to Invest in a Portfolio

Once you have accessed the equity in your property, you have a couple of different options to make an investment portfolio. You can work with a financial advisor at small boutique firms all the way up to large name-brand firms. The financial advisor helps you choose the investment options that will help you meet your goals. With a check in hand, you can open up a brokerage account with one of these firms and be on your way to investing.

You can also choose to take your investment journey on your own. Some of the same firms that offer financial advisors also offer self-directed accounts where you can manage your account by phone or via the Internet. There are also online investment firms that do not have brick-and-mortar establishments. If you choose to go it alone, the account fees and management fees are usually lower than those managed by a financial advisor because you will have to do your own research and trades (buying and selling of your investments), rather than paying a financial advisor to do it for you. The time you may have to spend getting up to speed on what you should invest in and then conducting the trades yourself may outweigh the fee you would pay to have a financial advisor to do it for you. Whether you choose to open and manage the account through a financial advisor or on your own, opening and investing in these types of accounts usually involve completing some paperwork and depositing the amount of equity you want to invest in order to fund the investment account.

When you invest in stocks, bonds, and mutual funds, there are a couple of ways you receive a return on your investment. In the case of bonds, you saw that you receive semi-annual interest payments until your bond matures. Depending on the stocks and mutual funds, your investment may also pay dividend and interest payments. Although the bonds have a yield rate that is set at the beginning of the investment, there is no guarantee on the rate of return you may receive on stocks and mutual funds.

If your stocks and mutual funds increase in value, you will not receive the return on your investment until you sell. On the other hand, if you sell when your investments are lower than what you paid for, then you are selling at a loss, meaning you have lost some of the principal investment amount and have not earned a return.

CASE STUDY: ACROSS THE BOARD INVESTMENTS

Ed Conarchy
Mortgage Planner
Cherry Creek Mortgage Company
945 Lakeview Parkway, Suite 170
Vernon Hills, IL 60061
www.edconarchy.com

As a professional mortgage planner, Ed Conarchy has helped client after client to leverage home equity funds to help them meet financial needs. From his years of experience working in the mortgage industry, when it came time for Conarchy to make some personal financial decisions of his own, he too decided to use his own home equity to make a variety of investments.

When Conarchy decided to pull some equity out of the home, the real estate market was at the top, and his primary residence was worth about $625,000. With an existing mortgage balance of approximately $350,000, he had a substantial amount of equity sitting in the home.

After reading a book and watching a DVD by financial advisor, author, and syndicated talk show host Ric Edelman, a light bulb went off in Conarchy's head. Rather than sit on this pile of money, he decided to pull the equity from his home and make it work for him. His first investment with the equity funds was to put a down payment on the purchase of a lake house that he and his family could use as a second or vacation home. Conarchy's investments did not stop there. He used some of the additional equity funds to remodel the basement of his primary residence. Not only did this allow him and his family to enjoy more livable space in their home, but it also added value to the property in the process.

With the rest of the home equity funds Conarchy had pulled out of his primary residence, he invested in a portfolio of equity funds, bond funds, real estate investment trusts (REITs), gold commodities, and more. This move created a more balanced, diversified, and liquid position to prepare Conarchy and his family for retirement, for paying his children's college education expenses, and for the unknown happenings and events that life may bring his way.

Checklist	
✓	Decide which type of investments and their associated risks match your goals
✓	Determine how much money you have to invest
✓	Determine which mixture of investments diversifies your portfolio to reach your investment goals

INVESTING
GROWTH
Techn
MONEY
TREASURY
STOCKS
Thri
Economy

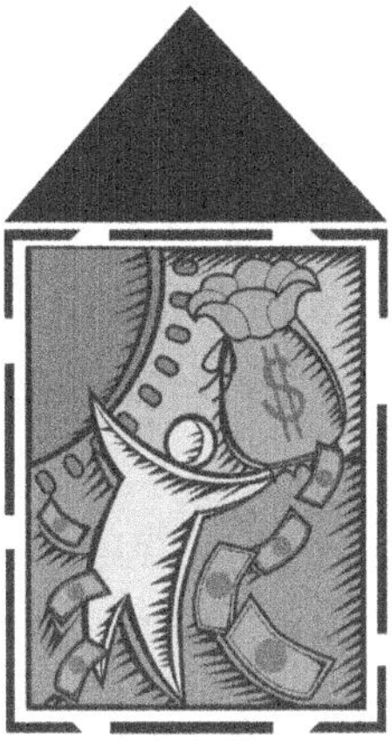

CONCLUSION

So to this point, you have learned that there are many ways to invest your hard-earned money. You now know that what may be right for your friend or neighbor may not be the right investment for you. You now have a full view of how investing the money from the equity in your home or real estate property can earn you a return on your investment, and which investment options will help you meet your financial goals. Whether you are planning for your retirement, trying to create cash flow from real estate investments, or buying insurance to protect the assets you own, you now have a more educated view of what investment options are available to you. Thoroughly researching your investment options – considering both the advantages and disadvantages – helps you to make the right investment options to fit your needs.

You have to take the opportunities you have available today to plan for tomorrow. This means you have to leverage the money today to fund tomorrow. If you own real estate, then you have learned that this is one of the sources of money you can use to invest as a means to create a better tomorrow. You can use this equity today to begin building a more stable financial future by investing in additional real estate properties; investing in a stock, bond, and mutual fund portfolio; funding a retirement account; or looking into any of the additional ways mentioned in this book.

The investment options you learned about in this book can help you understand the value of the money you invest. Do not put yourself in a position where you use the equity funds available to you by making purchases in depleting assets that do not provide you a return on your investment or provide so small a return that it does not help you meet your financial goals. Take what you have learned to invest your equity funds wisely – in ways you can enjoy the appreciation rather than the depletion of the money you have invested. You have the information you need to conduct further research and learn how to leverage the equity buildup in your real estate property or business to plan for your future. Take this information and do what you need to create a better financial future for you and your family.

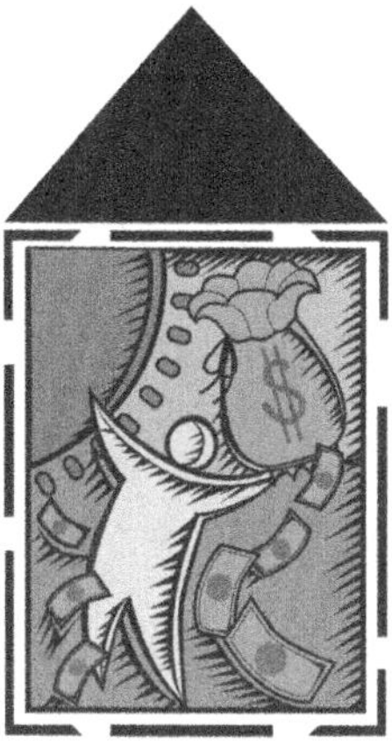

RESOURCES

Bank Rate: **www.bankrate.com**

Small Business Administration (SBA): **www.sba.gov**

Internal Revenue Service: **www.irs.gov**

Bill Savings: **www.billsavings.com**

Insurance Information Institute: **www.iii.org**

Social Security Administration: **www.ssa.gov**

Life Happens: **www.lifehappens.org**

Financial Aid: **www.finaid.org**

Remodeling Magazine: **www.remodeling.hw.net**

Broker Outpost: **www.brokeroutpost.com/reference/30514.htm**

Mortgage 101: **www.mortgage101.com/article/balloon-mortgages**

Investor Words: **www.investorwords.com**

College Board: **www.collegeboard.com**

THE UNITED STATES OF AMERICA
RESERVE NOTE
RESERVE

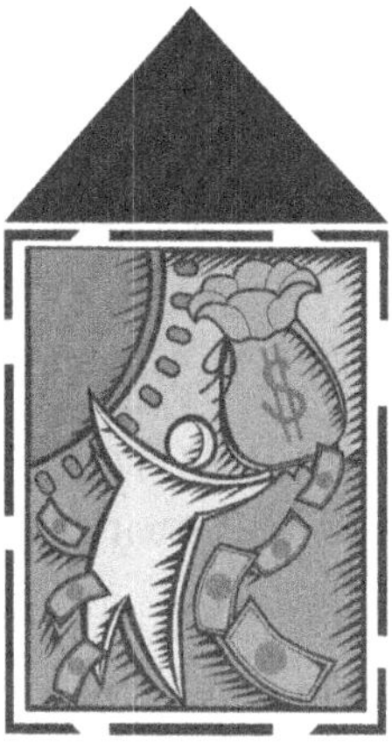

GLOSSARY

Adjustable-Rate Mortgage (ARM): An adjustable-rate mortgage is also known as a variable-rate mortgage. Directly opposite of a fixed-rate mortgage, the interest rate on an ARM adjusts or changes periodically.

Adjustment Period: The time period established for an adjustable-rate mortgage interest rate to change. For example, if the adjustment period on a mortgage is one year, then the interest rate is due to adjust once a year.

Amortization: Gradually paying off the mortgage debt by making equal principal and interest payments on a monthly basis until the debt is completely repaid.

Annual Percentage Rate (APR): The annualized cost of borrowing money that not only takes the interest rate of the mortgage into consideration, but also factors in closing costs. The APR represents the true cost of credit and is the best way to compare one loan to another to see which option is truly the lowest cost, regardless of the interest rate.

Appraisal: Determines the estimated market value of a property.

Balloon Mortgage: A mortgage with a fixed interest rate and monthly payment for a short period (usually less than five years). At the end of the fixed rate period, the balance of the mortgage comes due, or "balloons." Balloon mortgage holders typically refinance into a new mortgage at the end of a balloon mortgage.

Bi-weekly Mortgage: A mortgage payment schedule where 50 percent of the monthly payment is paid every two weeks. It is equivalent to making one extra mortgage payment per year because the loan amortization is faster, as it reduces the amount of interest that accrues.

Bond: A debt instrument issued by the U.S. government, an organization, or other institution to raise money – typically for a specific project.

Borrower (Mortgagor): The party or parties who apply for a mortgage to finance the purchase or refinance of real estate property and are responsible for repaying the loan (mortgage) to the lender.

Bridge Loan: An interim loan taken out on the current residence that the owner uses to fund the purchase of a new property. Once the borrower sells the home secured by the loan, the loan is paid off.

Buy Down: When the borrower on a mortgage pays additional points on the mortgage (each point equals 1 percent of the loan amount) to obtain a lower interest rate on the mortgage.

Bylaws: A set of regulations a condominium association sets and uses as a guideline to conduct association business.

Capital Gains: The amount of profit a property owner receives when the property is sold.

Cash Flow: The amount of money received as income for an investment property that is rented or leased to tenants. Positive cash flow occurs when there is enough income to cover the expenses of the property. The money that exceeds the expenses is profit. Negative cash flow is when the income from the property is not enough to cover the expenses of it.

Closing: When the ownership of a property is transferred from the seller to the buyer. This usually takes place at the office of the title company, attorney, or real estate agent's office involved in the transaction.

Closing Costs: Costs associated with a real estate transaction (purchase or refinance) when mortgage financing is involved. In a purchase situation, there are closing costs that the buyer is responsible for and closing costs that the seller are responsible for paying. Some of the costs associated with closing a real estate transaction include an origination fee or discount points, underwriting, processing, document preparation, flood certification, tax service, title insurance, escrows, attorney fees, recording fees, inspection, appraisal, and real estate agent commission.

Commitment: A written statement from the lender of a mortgage saying it agrees to extend a mortgage on a property under specific terms and conditions to the borrower.

Conditional Commitment: A written statement from the lender of a mortgage saying it agrees to extend a mortgage on a property under specific terms and conditions to the borrower, as long as certain conditions are met prior to closing.

Condominium: A residential building or complex where individuals own the individual units, but there is an association and bylaws that govern the common areas and facilities the unit owners share.

Construction Loan: A mortgage that covers the costs of building a home. Rather than disburse the entire project at once, construction loans typically disburse payments to the builder of the home in draws as milestones are met on the project. When the construction of the home is complete, permanent mortgage arrangements must be made to pay off the construction loan.

Contingency: Conditions outlined in the purchase contract or in the mortgage commitment that the buyer or borrower must meet before the closing.

Contract: A legally binding agreement between the seller and buyer of a property. In order for an agreement to be valid, legal, and binding in a real estate transaction, the agreement must contain:

1. An offer
2. An acceptance
3. Competent parties

4. Consideration (monetary value)
5. Legal purpose
6. Written documentation
7. Description of the property
8. Signatures by principals or their attorney-in-fact

Conventional Loan: Any type of conforming or non-conforming mortgage that is not a VA or FHA loan.

Credit Report: A detailed report listing the credit history of a borrower, including types of accounts, account balances, and payment history, which is reported to the credit agency by the creditor or can be found in public records.

Deed: A written and legally binding document that transfers the ownership of real estate property from the seller to the buyer. In order for the document to be legally binding and valid, it must contain an accurate description of the property being transferred, signed, and witnessed by the parties involved in accordance with the laws of the state where the property stands and given to the buyer at the time of closing.

Deed of Trust: Legal instrument used in many states as security to receive payment on the loan note. A deed of trust is used in these states rather than use a mortgage to secure the payment of a note. Three parties are involved in this type of transaction: a borrower, a trustee, and a lender. A borrower transfers title of the property to a trustee. A trustee holds the property in trust as security to receive payment on the loan note for the lender. When the borrower pays the debt as agreed, the deed of trust becomes void. If the borrower defaults, the trustee can sell the property without a court proceeding.

Depreciation: A decline in the value of real estate because of wear and tear, obsolescence, adverse changes in the neighborhood, or any other reason.

Documentary Tax Stamps: Stamps attached to a deed that represent the amount of the tax that was paid during the transfer of ownership on the property.

Down Payment: The amount of money paid for the purchase of a property that is excluded from the mortgage amount or any closing costs.

Earnest Money: This may also be referred to as a good faith deposit and is the amount of money a buyer deposits into an escrow account when making a bid to buy a piece of real estate. This money is typically applied toward the down payment when the sale and purchase agreement is complete.

Equity: Value after reducing the market value of the home or building by the amount of loans, mortgages, or other liens on the property.

Escrow: Account held by a neutral third party in a real estate transaction that handles all of the funds between the buyer and the seller. The buyer of a property deposits funds into the escrow account, and the mortgage lender funds the loan through the escrow account. The neutral third-party escrow account holder then disburses the funds to pay for real estate agent commissions, to pay off any old loans and liens against the property, pay real estate taxes and any other fees associated with the transaction, and provide the funds due to the seller.

Federal National Mortgage Association (FNMA, Fannie Mae): A government agency that purchases loans from lenders, guarantees the loans to protect the lender from default, packages these mortgages into mortgage-backed securities (MBS), and sells MBS to investors.

Federal Home Loan Mortgage Corporation (FHLMC, Freddie Mac): An agency that purchases loans from Federal Reserve and Federal Home Loan Bank Systems members, guarantees the loans to protect the lender from default, packages these mortgages into mortgage backed securities (MBS), and sells MBS to investors.

Federal Housing Administration (FHA): A government agency that is part of the U.S. Department of Housing and Urban Development (HUD) , which provides loan programs and issues loan guarantees to make homeownership more readily available.

Federal Reserve System: Governing body responsible for the federal monetary policy, which includes regulating and providing services to commercial banks that are members of the federal banking system.

Finance Charge: Interest charged to a borrower by a lender.

First Mortgage: A mortgage that is in first position on a piece of property. The order of the mortgage determines how obligations are paid on the property in the case of a sale or default. A first mortgage takes priority for repayment of the debt.

Free and Clear: A property that does not have any mortgages or liens.

Hazard Insurance: Coverage on real estate that insures against various risks, which typically include fire, theft, and liability.

Homeowner's Association: The governing body of a housing development or condominium to manage and enforce the common areas of the development, as well as the association rules and regulations.

Homestead: Status of a home when it is the primary residence. In some states, a homestead property is protected against bankruptcy and other judgments.

Homestead Exemption: A reduction in the market value of a primary residence for the purpose of calculating property tax. Only available in some states, it gives the homeowner a break on the amount he or she pays in taxes.

Housing and Urban Development: A government agency that oversees some federal housing and community development programs, such as FHA.

HUD 1: A federally required document that discloses an itemized list of closing costs to the buyer before closing.

Improvements: Any additions or renovations that add value to a raw piece of land. Some examples include building a home or building and paving streets.

Index: Indicator of the current financial situation in the economy, which is used as the base rate for determining interest rate adjustments on variable-rate mortgages.

Lien: A claim made against property for a debt such as a mortgage, judgment, or payment of taxes.

Loan Application: A document used by mortgage lenders to collect specific personal and financial information on the borrower and information about the property. The lender uses the document as the basis for processing the mortgage for approval or denial.

Loan Origination Fee or Points: Fee charged by the mortgage lender or broker for originating a loan. Each point equals 1 percent of the mortgage amount.

Loan-to-Value Ratio (LTV): The percentage the mortgage lender loans on the amount of the purchase price or market value of the property, whichever of the two figures is lower.

Loan Servicing: Actions taken on a mortgage after it closes, such as collecting monthly mortgage payments, managing property tax and insurance escrows, paying property taxes and insurance, and foreclosing on defaulted loans.

Margin: The number added to an index to calculate the interest rate in a variable-rate mortgage.

Market Value: The going price that a property could sell for at any given point in time. For mortgage purposes, the mortgage lender typically uses the appraised value of a property to determine market value.

Mortgage: A written debt instrument, which places a lien on the piece of real estate, turning the real state into the security for the loan.

Mortgage Backed Security (MBS): A pool of mortgage loans sold as a bond or other financial obligation.

Mortgage Banker: The role of a specialist at a bank that originates and services mortgages. Some mortgage banking institutions provide loan servicing, while others turn the mortgages over to servicing companies.

Mortgage Broker: A professional mortgage originator who acts as a liaison between the mortgage borrower and the mortgage lender. In return for arranging the financing between a borrower and a lender, the broker is paid a fee, which is usually a set percentage of the mortgage amount, at the time of closing.

Mortgagee: The mortgage lender.

Mortgagor: The mortgage borrower.

Mortgage Note: A written debt agreement secured by a mortgage, which includes the repayment details, such as the amount of the debt, and the manner in which the debt must be repaid.

Negative Amortization: When the interest portion of the monthly mortgage payment is not enough to cover the true cost of interest. The amount of interest not paid is then added to the principal balance of the mortgage.

Note: A written debt instrument a borrower signs to acknowledge the debt and his or her responsibility to repay the debt.

PITI: An acronym used for the principal, interest, taxes, and insurance payment for a mortgage payment.

Points: Fees paid to a lender for the origination and processing of a mortgage. Each point equals 1 percent of the mortgage amount. Points can be sub-divided into origination points or discount points.

Portfolio Loan: A mortgage retained for servicing by a bank or lender rather than being sold to investors on the secondary market.

Prepaid Interest: The prepayment by the borrower of interest fees due for the portion of the month they own the property. This interest is paid at the time of closing. This type of interest is typically calculated for the mortgage, taxes, and insurance on the property.

Prepayment: When a borrower pays the principal balance due before the end of the term of the mortgage, which may occur from additional mortgage payments, a payoff of the mortgage when the property sells, or the borrower's refinancing into a new mortgage.

Prepayment Penalty: A penalty fee paid by the borrower when a mortgage balance is paid before the end of the term of the mortgage, or before the prepayment time period established by the lender at the time the mortgage is established. For example, a 30-year mortgage may have a prepayment penalty for the first two years. If the borrower pays off the principal balance within the first two years, then the lender may charge a prepayment penalty fee, which is typically a percentage of the mortgage balance.

Prime Rate: The interest rate that the most creditworthy borrowers are charged by a commercial bank.

Principal: The outstanding balance due on a loan.

Private Mortgage Insurance (PMI): A fee charged to protect a mortgage lender when they loan a borrower a higher amount because the borrower puts less than a 20 percent down payment on the purchase of a property, or the equity is less than 20 percent for a refinance. This fee is paid by the borrower and is typically added to the monthly mortgage payment collected by the mortgage lender or servicing company.

Property Tax: Fee based on the market value of the property, which is collected by the county where the property is located.

Realtor: A real estate professional who is a member of the National Association of Realtors and helps buyers and sellers of real estate to complete transactions.

Real Estate Broker: The individual real estate company owner or manager of the real estate office that holds a brokerage license to represent a buyer or a seller in a real estate transaction.

Real Estate Settlement Procedure Act (RESPA): A federal law that regulates the actions, steps, and procedures a mortgage lender must take when dealing with mortgage loans for any real estate property up to four units (not commercial properties).

Refinancing: Establishing a new mortgage or loan to pay off an existing mortgage or loan on the same piece of property.

Recording: The entering of a debt instrument such as a mortgage into the public records. A mortgage or deed of trust is entered into the public records as proof of the debt on the property.

Regulation Z (Reg Z): A federal regulation that requires lenders fully disclose the terms of a loan, including the annual percentage rate (APR).

Real Estate Investment Trusts (REIT): A trust established to purchase and manage real estate utilizing investors' money. Investors typically receive realize some tax advantages for owning real estate when they invest in this type of trust.

Second Home: A home that is not the primary residence but is used as a vacation home. This home cannot be rented out, or it is considered an investment property.

Second Mortgage: A mortgage that takes second-lien position on the property behind the first mortgage. Generally, these mortgages have higher interest rates than first mortgages, as they represent a higher risk for an investor because when a property is sold or foreclosed upon, second mortgages get paid only after the first mortgage is paid in full.

Timeshare: A form of property ownership in which numerous people own and have rights to the property for a certain amount of time each year. Usually used for vacation properties.

Title: Proof of ownership of a property.

Title Insurance: A type of insurance policy established to protect the buyer and lender on a property against loss from defects in title.

Title Report: A document provided by the title company in a real estate transaction, which details the current ownership, outstanding deeds of trust or mortgages, liens, easements, covenants, restrictions, and defects on the property.

Title Search: Typically performed by the title company involved in a real estate transaction to see what ownership and lien information the public records show for the property in question.

Townhouse: A type of residential home that shares walls with at least one other unit, which typically has two or more floors in each unit. These types of residences are commonly found in planned unit developments (PUDs) and condominiums.

Triple-Net Lease: A type of commercial lease in which the tenant is responsible for all operating expenses of the property, while the landlord receives the rent payment.

Zoning: Governs how a property can be used: residentially, commercially or agriculturally. The city or county where the property is located typically determines zoning.

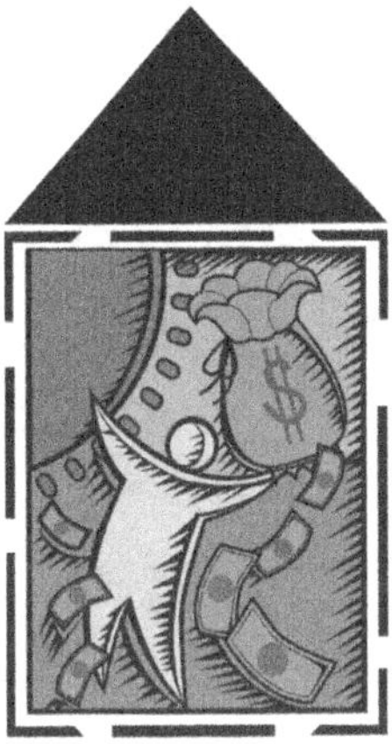

BIBLIOGRAPHY

Tyson, Eric. *Personal Finance for Dummies.* Indianapolis: Wiley Publishing Inc., 2006.

Snow, Marian. *Stop Sitting on Your Assets.* Chicago: Ethan Madison Publishing, 2007.

Cummings, Jack. *The Real Estate Investor's Guide to Cash Flow and Equity Management.* Hoboken: Wiley Publishing Inc., 2006.

Hitesman, Pete. *The Insider's Guide to Home Equity Borrowing.* Dublin: Relentless Press, 2004.

DeFrancesco, Roccy. *The Home Equity Acceleration Plan.* St. Joseph: TriArc Advisors, LLC, 2008.

DeFrancesco, Roccy. *How to Achieve Maximum Wealth with Maximum Security.* St. Joseph: TriArc Advisors, LLC, 2008.

Mobius, Mark. *Equities: An Introduction to the Core Concepts.* Singapore: John Wiley & Sons, 2007.

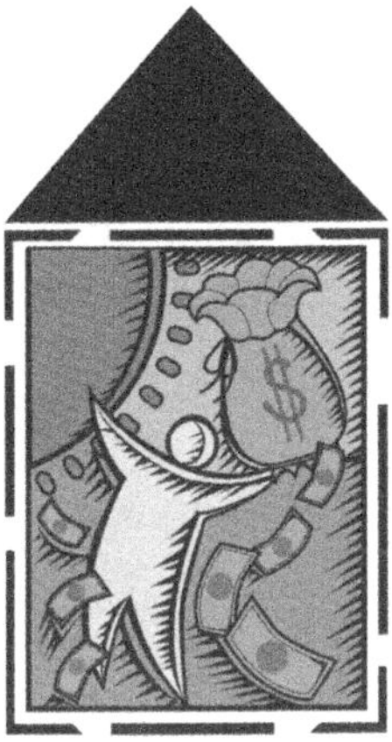

BIOGRAPHY

Kristie Lorette

Kristie Lorette is a copywriter who specializes in finance, real estate, marketing, event planning, mortgages, and nonprofits. After a six-year career with Merrill Lynch, Lorette founded and operated her own event-planning business for four years. Lorette then returned to the corporate world working in marketing for a mortgage and finance company, later for a real estate attorney, and finally for a history museum. She now uses her experience marketing and writing in these industries to help businesses, organizations, and entrepreneurs create copy and marketing collateral that sizzles, motivates, and sells.

LIBERTY

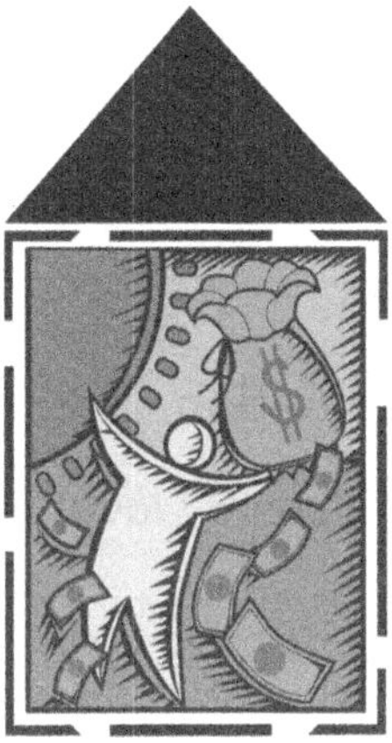

INDEX

D

E

F

H

I

L

M

N

P

R

S

T

Z

Made in United States
North Haven, CT
11 November 2026

22197183R00163